MW01235308

Seeking Simplicity:

A Woman's Guide to a Balanced Life

By

Elizabeth Gregory

© 2002 by Elizabeth Gregory. All rights reserved.

No part of this book may be reproduced, stored in a retrieval system, or transmitted by any means, electronic, mechanical, photocopying, recording, or otherwise, without written permission from the author.

ISBN: 1-4033-0118-2 (Ebook)
ISBN: 1-4033-0119-0 (Softcover)

This book is printed on acid free paper.

All scripture quotations are taken from the New King James Version copyright 1983 by Thomas Nelson, Inc.

1stBooks - rev. 5/3/02

Dedications

I am thankful to my heavenly Father that He continues to guide me through this journey of life.

I thank all the women, named and unnamed that have nourished my spiritual growth.

My gratitude also goes to my husband who has encouraged my work and accepted my preoccupation with the writing of this book without complaint.

Table of Contents

Introduction

I am not writing this book as an expert with my life neatly ordered in little compartments and organized to the hilt. I am writing as a fellow traveler along this journey of life with its disorder, chaos, constant demands and ever-changing tides. I have struggled with the demands of education and career while raising a family. I have, at various passages, been a wife and mother, a step-mom and single parent. I understand the struggles that divorced women and single Moms face. Now my nest is empty and I am in a wonderfully satisfying marriage that is nothing short of a miraculous gift from God. My daughter is now grown and has two children of her own, making me happily a grandmother as well.

I do not write this book as the perfect Christian telling others how to live. I am a sinner, in need of God's redeeming work through His son, Jesus, the Christ. I am a prodigal daughter who experienced God's grace and love in my life. He has given me far more than I could ever deserve. It is a frightening prospect to open up one's life to the degree I have done in the following pages. It is only my faith that my journey may be helpful to others that allows me to do so.

Why write a book about seeking simplicity in life? The changes in my life have been constant. I found myself saying, "My life will be easier when...she can feed herself, she can dress herself, she starts kindergarten, she goes to school, she gets a little older, she can drive, she finishes high school." It seemed I was always waiting for some future time when life would just miraculously get simpler. Well, life never did just get easier on its' own. Even in an empty house with only me, myself and I, I was feeling pushed, pressured and hurried to do something more with my life. That's when I decided, the busyness in life was not caused by something out there, but by me. I was doing this to myself! I needed to do a little soul searching. I now realize that the process of simplifying my life is anything but simple. If you decide to read on, you may be facing one of the most difficult challenges in your lifetime.

Seeking simplicity is going against everything our popular culture teaches us. It is being courageous enough to say, "I don't have to have it all, enough is enough!" It is a decision to evaluate life on your own terms and set your priorities, and deciding for yourself what deems you a success. Complexity is normal in life, simplicity takes effort. So, if you are up to the challenge, read on. I trust you will find your soul and your creator in the process that I have set down in these pages. I speak from the framework of a committed Christian who has taken many wrong turns in this journey of life. I speak also as a professional counselor and a clinical specialist in nursing with over twenty-eight years of working with women who struggle to be all things to all people and have experienced burnout or depression in the process.

I share my journey and experience with you now because I find that women are hungry for this experience. You will also read part of the journeys of other women within the pages of this book. I pray you will find this a meaningful journey.

Seeking Simplicity is written as a self-assessment tool and workbook. I encourage you to do the exercises as you come to them. Later exercises build upon the earlier ones. As with anything in life, you will only get back what you put into this process. Before beginning, write down what it would mean for you to live a more simplified life. What led you to pick up this book and begin to read?

Chapter One

Where Do I Start?

Matthew 6:33
But seek first the kingdom of God, and his righteousness, and
all these things shall be added unto you.

We spend so much energy seeking acceptance by others in our society. Perhaps, if we return to Christ's teaching to seek God first, we will have taken the first step toward simplifying life. What is the first step in this process?

Start by taking a deep breath, then schedule some time for yourself. You may need only thirty minutes to an hour a day, or you may want a whole week-end to just read through this book in one sitting, then go back and do one chapter at a time. You may choose to work this book alone or with a small group of women. If you work together, you also get the benefit of one another's experience and wisdom. I prefer to teach this material in a two day retreat, so that the participants have a chance to pull away from all the usual daily demands and listen closely to what God is teaching them. There are checklists and questions to complete as you go through the book. This process helps you apply the principles to your current life situation.

We need to begin by defining what it is we are striving for. Simplicity is defined in the Merriam-Webster Dictionary as "the state of being simple, uncomplicated, or uncompounded". It is further defined as "freedom from pretense or guile" and "directness of expression". The first definition is what you will find in most books on time management and organization skills in an attempt to simplify life. This book refers more to the latter definitions. I am not writing about simple techniques, I am writing about clarifying the priorities and essentials of a meaningful life.

Anne Morrow Lindbergh shared her experience of finding simplicity in her book, <u>Gift From The Sea</u> written in 1955 in this way. "The pattern of our lives is essentially circular. We must be open to all points of the compass; husband, children, friends, home, community; stretched out, exposed, sensitive like a spider's web to each breeze that blows, to each call that comes. How difficult for us, then, to achieve a balance in the midst of these contradictory tensions, and yet how necessary for the proper functioning of our lives." I first read these words in 1982 after the book was released again in 1975 and have re-read this treasure of a book every year since. She clearly understood the tensions in a woman's life as we are called on by a variety of loved ones and roles to fulfill. This tension existed even in the1950's, which we now see as a simpler time.

Now, how do you start to find your own meaning in life?

Step One: Ask, "Who Am I?". Chances are you are someone's wife, someone's mother, someone's daughter, friend to many, church leader, community volunteer, political activist, someone's employee, possibly someone's boss, and on and on and on. We as women, tend to define ourselves by the roles we play in the lives of the people we love. However, imagine for a few minutes, that the worst nightmare of your life occurs, and suddenly all the other people in your life cease to exist. You are utterly and completely alone. Now, who are you? Let this sink in. You still exist even though all your relationships and roles cease. Who are you? What do you believe in? What has any meaning in life?

I experienced a time of changes almost this drastic once in reality. Not all the roles ended, but a traumatic divorce left me without a husband, without two step-sons I had dearly loved for eight years, without my standing in the community, without close friends, without church support, and without any sense of where to go from there. In addition, everything I ever believed about God was up for grabs. That sense of lost-ness and broken-ness was the start of my journey.

I was still a mom. I was still employed, yet needing other employment if I was going to keep a roof over our heads. I was also confused, depressed, lonely and terrified. I felt ashamed and unworthy of God's attention, so I even shut Him out. I survived and I became a whole new creation as I learned who I am, not who the world told me I was.

Take a minute and answer the question: Who Am I? How do you define yourself?

How much of this self-definition is based on the relationships in your life? How much on the roles you fulfill? How else can you define yourself? Try this. Go through the following checklist and see which words and interests describe you.

____ a lover of nature   ____ a woman of faith

____ an appreciator of art   ____ a lover of music

____ a woman of style   ____ an amusing companion

____ a woman of wisdom   ____ a gourmet cook

____ quick witted, humorous   ____ creative

____ sensitive, insightful   ____ understanding

___ patient   ___ loving

___ thoughtful, kind   ___ organized

___ athletic, active   ___ adventurous

___ curious   ___ outgoing

___ introspective   ___ encouraging

___ artistic   ___ domestic

Do you get the idea now? You may well be the most wonderful and exciting woman you know. How is anyone else going to know that if you don't even know it yourself?

Step Two: Get back in touch with the girl you once were. Look back at age eight, twelve, fifteen, and nineteen. What were your dreams? Did you dream of being a pilot, an artist, a writer, an actress, a nurse, a teacher, a mother, a wife? Were your dreams defined on the relationships you hoped for or on experiences you hoped would come your way?

What were your dreams?

How many of these dreams have you realized? If any have not been actualized in your life so far, what has kept you from realizing them?

Do you believe you still have a chance at reaching any of these long forgotten dreams? Choose one dream from your childhood and promise yourself you won't let it die. As you go through the process described in this book, see where your dream can fit in.

Step three: What are the values that guide you in your life? Where did you learn these? Is your life dictated by the values we are taught through our mass media? There is a plethora of commercials, movies and books that teach us we have to be rich, slim, famous or remarkable in some way. Those of us who are average, common people, and that is most of us, are left with the idea that we and our lives are uninteresting and of little value to others. The feeling of unimportance may cause us to ask, "How could God use plain little ole me?" The failure to understand that God created you to be just who you are may keep you from realizing that you are important to Him and He desires your life to glorify Him. All through the scriptures, God used everyday people to do great things. The power comes from Him. Think a few minutes about all we are taught is important in a woman's life.

Use this checklist to help you identify these values that underlie your sense of who you are. Write in others.

_____ honest		_____ beautiful	
_____ responsible		_____ financially independent	
_____ wealthy		_____ community leader	
_____ spiritual		_____ religious	
_____ church leader		_____ successful	
_____ athletic		_____ teacher	
_____		_____	

As you complete the checklist, you will find there are other words that need clearer definition. Just as simplicity means different things to various people, so do words like success, leadership, spirituality, financial stability and beauty. Success may mean wealth and independence with the ability to travel and own valuable property to one woman. It may mean an ability to be content with what you have to another. Success has come to mean an ability to define my life by what I feel

God is calling me to do. This has meant letting go of material possessions, activities, committees, and even further formal education so I could become still and know God as I sought His direction for my life.

In many books on leadership by motivational writers, success seems to be defined as reaching one's maximum potential based on the amount of money earned and the widespread ability to influence others. I warn you to be cautious about buying into our societal tendency to equate success with income. A highly self-actualized and successful first grade teacher will earn far less money than a self centered and verbally abusive surgeon. Yet is her work any less meaningful? Does she contribute any less to the good of society? I think not! The jobs with the strongest sense of purpose and service to others are generally the occupations that pay a modest salary. Teachers, ministers, counselors, social workers, nurses, and yes, even mothers share of themselves and improve our society every day. These are the occupations that develop service minded young adults. These adults of tomorrow are the future of our society. Quite honestly, can you think of a more important job than being a loving 'Mom'? Raising our children to contribute to the future world and serve our God has to be the most important work we can do. Yet, stay-at-home Moms frequently feel they have to explain their choice to be at home and often feel judged by others for failing to live up to their potential.

Leadership is defined in the dictionary as "the office or position" and "the capacity to lead". Leadership is the ability to motivate others by example. True leaders rise to the top repeatedly because they have an indescribable ability to encourage and teach others. A leader recognizes the potential in each individual and encourages that person to grow. Leadership is not bossing others around and insisting on being in control. This also applies to parenting. Some parents are natural leaders that motivate their children through encouragement. Others boss their children around and demand respect. Which is the more successful approach?

In John 10:3-4, Jesus is described as the shepherd who leads His sheep in this way, "To him the doorkeeper opens, and the sheep hear his voice; and he calls his own sheep by name and leads them out. And when he brings out his own sheep, he goes before them; and the sheep follow him, for they know his voice." What a beautiful description this is of leadership. He does not issue forth orders and demands. He invites us to journey with Him. In that journey, we come to know Christ, ourselves and our fellow humankind. Do we trust Him enough to follow him out of the gate of the world's values?

Beautiful is truly a loaded word in our society with examples of beauty as anorexic young women and pumped up young men. Although there has been an outcry against this stereotype, the movies, television programs and advertising industries insist on portraying beauty in this way. Most of us have matured enough to know that being physically healthy, caring for our bodies, remaining active, and developing healthy relationships are far better measures of beauty. Yet plastic surgery is keeping a lot of people rich. There are times when modifying our physical body may have a positive effect on the well-being of a person. It is appropriate for reconstruction after burns or injuries or correcting a deformity that has left a child feeling undeserving of love. If our society did not place so much emphasis on physical beauty to start with, even these would be less important. Take a moment and think about a woman in your life that you would describe as being truly beautiful. What features or characteristics cause you to see her in this way?

Do you meet your own definition of beauty? If not, what is missing from within? What changes would be needed to allow you to see your own unique beauty?

Now that you've had some time to think it through... Who are you? Write another description of yourself. How does this differ from the first description?

Let's go further. It's time to assess your lifestyle, relationships, use of time, activities, finances and material possessions. As we begin, name the obstacles that you believe are holding you back from having the simplified and purposeful life you desire.

Chapter Two

Where Does All The Time Go?

Ecclesiastes 3:1-8
To everything there is a season,
A time to every purpose under heaven:
A time to be born, And a time to die;
A time to plant, And a time to pluck what is planted;
A time to kill, And a time to heal;
A time to break down, And a time to build up;
A time to weep, And a time to laugh;
A time to mourn, And a time to dance;
A time to cast away stones, And a time to gather stones;
A time to embrace, And a time to refrain from embracing;
A time to gain, And a time to lose;
A time to keep, And a time to throw away;
A time to tear, And a time to sew;
A time to keep silence, And a time to speak;
A time to love, And a time to hate;
A time of war, And a time of peace.

We all complain about not having enough time, yet we are each given the same 24 hours a day, 60 minutes an hour, and 60 seconds a minute. Today is all we have. We may not be given the gift of tomorrow. The past is now past and we cannot change it. Acknowledge that in every life there is indeed, a time for sorrow, for grieving, for letting go and for joy. Maybe now is the time for you to let go of the past so you can embrace the gift of this day.

Seasons of Life

There are seasons throughout our lives and a time for every thing. One of the advantages to getting older (yes, there are some advantages), is that we can begin to see how the seasons flow into one another. Until you feel great sorrow, you cannot fully appreciate great joy. There are seasons of birth in our own ideals, in relationships and in desires. There are deaths when beliefs are proven wrong and ideals were based on erroneous teachings. We see the promise of a new relationship and later witness the hope for a lasting love die as it withers on the vine. It is through the births and deaths of various aspects of life that you can begin to comprehend the whole. Looking back at life, you can see how an event that occurred when you were nineteen has a profoundly positive effect on you at forty-five years of age. At age nineteen, however, it seemed you would never get over it and you could see no way that this event could possibly work toward a good purpose. There are times to repair a damaged friendship, and a time for letting one go. There are times to extend ourselves, acknowledge our faults, admit our wrongs against others, and seek understanding, compassion and forgiveness.

Some women have shared their insights gained through this journey of life:

One of Jody's favorite phrases is "This too shall pass". "When I start feeling overwhelmed or out-of-control in life circumstances, it helps to remember that this time or problem will pass. It will not last forever. In a few days, weeks, or even years, this problem will be a thing of the past."

Sara shared her understanding of the "wages of sin". "You take the phrase, 'the wages of sin is death' and tend to see this only as a loss of saving grace for the eternal soul if we refuse to let go of our sin and submit to the Lordship of Christ. I have come to see this in a more daily and personal way. When I lie to a friend, their trust in me dies. When I betray another who loves me, the relationship can never be the same. The level of intimacy is destroyed. When I refuse to wait on the Lord for guidance, my mistakes will lead to my own destructiveness. The scripture isn't meant only for the saving of our eternal soul, but as a map for our daily interactions with others as well."

Gini struggled with doubts about her faith in God when her oldest child was in first grade and she had not received the answers she hoped for from prayers that her unbelieving husband would come to accept Christ. She had an experience one bleak January day in which she felt a separation from everyone, including God. "It was a bitterly cold day in Illinois. The wind chill factor was minus 20 degrees and the remains of the last snow lay on the ground. The snow was tinged with black and everything in our backyard looked desolate and gray. I remember crying as I looked out the family room window. My breath made frost marks on the window panes. I asked God why my life seemed so much like my backyard appeared. I felt alone and was desperate for companionship from my husband. I told the Lord that I felt like the cherry tree in the center of my wintry scene...bleak and frozen. I felt I was out on a limb (not the Shirley McClaine type of limb) all by myself. The Lord spoke very clearly to my spirit saying, "Out on the limb is where I will grow the fruit. Without the dead of winter the sap can't freeze. The same sap will flow again in the spring to form the fragrant blossoms that will miraculously form delicious, dark, bing cherries." She goes on to say, "I've reflected on that day many times and have seen God take me through the winters of my soul in order to grow blossoms and fruit in my life. Now I can thank Him even in the midst of problems, knowing that He is faithful to turn seemingly bad situations into something that will become a lovely fragrance in my life, simply because He loves me and is faithful to His covenant to be merciful to me." Gini now loves the bleak winters of Illinois and has come to understand the spiritual application of I Thessalonians 5:18 "in every thing give thanks: for this is the will of God in Christ Jesus concerning you."

There are seasons of great joy as we watch our children grow a little every day. The beauty of a child's curiosity and enthusiasm is inspirational to watch. Remember when you used to run just for the fun of running?

There are seasons when we feel overwhelmed by demands on our time. The middle years of raising children, maintaining a job, and keeping up a home is probably one of the the most challenging seasons of life. It is in this "oyster bed of life" as Anne Morrow Lindbergh called it, that we can lose ourselves. We extend all our resources to take care of others we love and have no time or energy left for ourselves. A relationship with God with the time for prayer and study can become a dim memory if we forget that He is the source of our strength. No matter what the season, even in a winter such as Gini has described, we can be comforted by the promise of Christ that He will always be with us, even to the ends of the world.

Managing the Time in our Days

Now let's look at time in it's simpler form. There are numerous books on time management. You already know the tricks about organizing your home, list making, and reducing steps in your kitchen to make the work easier. What is it that keeps us from being able to prioritize, to say "No" to unwanted activities and phone solicitations? I think that we, as women, are socialized from an early age to believe that our time is not really our own. Our role is to meet the needs of our husband, children, friends, church and community as others define for us what takes priority. Well, it's true. Our time is not our own. If we want to surrender our lives to God and serve Him, our time is not our own. It is His. We need to think twice before we frivolously give away God's time that He created in our lives to serve Him. If we are going to seek first the kingdom of God, then we must give of our time to Him and allow Him to prioritize where the rest of the time will be spent. Any relationship, including the one with our Heavenly Father requires time. Time spent together, time listening, and time sharing our own needs, concerns, and fears. We will look more closely at this issue in the chapters on relationships and spirituality.

Take a few minutes now to look at how you are using your time. In a typical weekday, where does your time go? Using the example as a guide, divide up your day by the way your spend your time:

Example	Your own

6-8 a.m. wake and dress

8-10 a.m. arrive at work, organize

10a.m.-12 noon work activity

12-1p.m. lunch

1-3p.m. meetings, paperwork

3-5p.m. complete work, close day

5-7p.m. return home, prepare dinner

7-9p.m. clean up at home

9-10p.m. time with family

10-11p.m. bath and bed

Now repeat the exercise for how your time is spent in an average weekend. List the entire 48 hours and see how you are using your time.

Friday evening: 6-8 p.m.

8-10p.m.

10-____

___-___ sleep

Saturday

6-8a.m.

8-10a.m.

10a.m.-12noon

12-2p.m.

2-4p.m.

4-6p.m.

6-8p.m.

8-10p.m.

10-__ p.m.

___-___ sleep

Sunday

6-8a.m.

8-10a.m.

10a.m.-12noon

12-2 p.m.

2-4p.m.

4-6p.m.

6-8p.m.

8-10p.m.

Are there any surprises? Are you spending the precious hours of each day fulfilling the demands of others? Are you claiming time for yourself to use in ways that enrich your life and allow creative expression?

Many women today have an additional responsibility that requires much time and energy...caring for aging parents. Women in their forties and fifties are often sandwiched between caring for two generations, their children at home and their own or their husband's parents. So where do we get the time we need for ourselves? When do we ever have time for Bible study or prayer? We cannot create more time. The answer lies in letting go of unnecessary activities, possessions, and unfulfilling relationships. Which of the things that eat up your time can be delegated to others? How can we accomplish worthwhile things with our time? Here are some ideas shared by other women just like us.

Sara learned that by splitting up the household chores into daily tasks, she could be free to enjoy her weekends more. "I started out doing the laundry on Thursdays. I'd put the first load in the washer before work, place it in the dryer as soon as I arrived home, then just keep a load going all evening. This was the chore that ate most of my time on Saturday morning and I wanted some free time. As my children got older, I taught them to help out. They could get the first load in the dryer when they got home from school, so we could get through earlier in the evening. It also taught them not to take clean clothes for granted." Sara went a step further. Her family learned to place dirty clothes in the hamper. Any clothes not there on Thursday simply did not get washed! The only exception was uniforms, as her daughter was a cheerleader and her son played soccer. These were washed after each use.

Jody shared how she became resentful that Saturday was a play day for everyone in the family except her. "It just wasn't fair. Every one else had two good eyes, two legs, and two hands. Why couldn't they do their share of the work? Then I realized, it was because I had never taught them to help. They saw housework as Mom's responsibility." Jody then held a family meeting and shared her frustrations. After teaching the children to do simple chores, it became a game for the family to meet in the kitchen on Saturday morning, set the timer, each get the list of chores assigned to them for that week, then take off. In one hour, everyone reconvened in the kitchen to share what chores had been completed. Another idea she had was to rotate the least enjoyable jobs. If one child hated to take out the trash, or empty the cat litterbox, it became a chore that rotated to a different person each week. "One other thing that really helped me was to spend twenty minutes a night picking up before we all got ready for bed. What a breath of fresh air it was to wake up in the morning to order, not chaos. Then, I could use that early morning time to take a walk, meditate or do something else that was calming to start my day."

"I found that I was wasting a lot of time moving paper around. The mail would get put on the table. I'd move it to the coffee table to set dinner out, then move it again to go through it. It just seemed to stack up. Newspapers are a nightmare. I honestly think they breed!", said Marie. She learned to go through the mail as soon as it arrived and throw out trash mail the first time through. Then she separated her mail from her husband's and set his stack on his desk. Then going through her own stack, things were handled one time and only one time. "Bills went into the folder for us to pay when we sit down at the end of the week, but that was the only thing I had to move twice." Newspapers were placed in a stack for unread issues, then when read were placed in a different stack and moved to the garage for recycling every two to three days. Marie learned that the same technique helped with e-mail and phone messages. Handle it at once and move on!

After simplifying tasks and delegating household work, you can apply all those time management techniques like cooking double and freeze half, keep a grocery list that the whole family adds to and make just one weekly trip to the store, and organize bathrooms, kitchens and closets. There are numerous books on the market to help you get a handle of techniques for time management. I'm more interested in how we have allowed all these chores to become the rulers of our lives and cause us to be out of balance.

Time and energy seem to go hand in glove. If we push ourselves relentlessly, we soon find we are chronically tired, irritable and generally dissatisfied with life. We are more likely to find fault with our husbands and see our children as spoiled. This carries over into work environments. When you are already tired when you get to work, it's hard to enjoy doing even more and meeting others' expectations. Getting adequate rest and eating a sensible diet are things we all know helps to increase energy. Exercise may be the most absent link for many women. Where do we find the time to add in taking care of ourselves? Some women find that waking a little earlier allows time to stretch and do some indoor exercise or take an early morning walk as the birds start to sing. Some find it easier to join with others at work to use the lunch break for walk time instead of sitting around and over-eating. Still others find a walk or bicycle ride in early evening helps reduce the strain of the day and helps them sleep better. The key here is priority. If you do not care for yourself, you will not be able to take care of those you love.

Elizabeth Gregory

By learning to simplify the use of our time and teaching our families to work together as a unit, we can create the space we need to allow God to renew our energy.

Stages of Life

There is another concept of time to look at a little closer. The stages of a woman's life require different responses. When children are very young, we cannot leave them behind to go for a quiet stroll unless Dad or a babysitter is available. They often follow us into the bathroom, for Pete's sake! Yet these stages of life do change. As you get older, you can learn to treasure the changes in each stage and season. Yes, young children keep us from sleeping through the night or spending time in solitude. But that time of life is so precious...and we can never go back. Our children grow up in a flash with ever changing needs. That art or dance class you want to take can be done, maybe just not today. List the things you want to learn and experience. Think how some of these may be shared with your children. Enjoy gardening together with your daughter or riding bicycles in early evening as a family. Play pitch with your son to get that upper body exercise. Thank God you have a toddler to race after as you shed the pounds accumulated during pregnancy. Count your blessings. I believe we really can have it

24

all...just not all at once! How can you apply this to your life now?

Activities I Want To Enjoy   How I Can Share These With Family

Time comes in minutes, hours, days and weeks. It comes in stages and seasons. It is one thing that is always moving and never returns. Time is similar to the flow of a river. It will keep flowing downstream. Sometimes it moves slowly and peacefully. Sometimes it is running wildly over large boulders and creating waves and eddies. Learning to adjust our activity load and expectations of ourselves to the flow of the river will help us manage time more effectively. In our current society, we all run at a breakneck pace on the average day. Then, with a crisis occurs, we do not have the energy to deal with things. We find that the irritability sets in and our relationships are damaged rather than strengthened during these trials of life. I encourage you to set yourself apart from the world long enough to discern what is important in this day, this stage or this season of your life. Allow God to set the priorities.

Chapter Three

Is All This Activity Really Necessary?

Acts 11:23
When he came, and had seen the grace of God, he was glad, and encouraged them all that with purpose of heart they should continue with the Lord.

The key words here are "with purpose". When we get honest with ourselves, we will see that much of our activity lacks purpose. It isn't just any activity that drains us of creative energy and robs us of our enthusiasm...it is purposeless activity. Activity with meaning increases our zest and joy for living. If we seek God's will in our lives above all else, then anything He wants us to do will have real meaning in our life or the lives of others.

Signs of Overload

What about managing stress created by being overly involved? Some stress is normal in life and it is quite unavoidable. Yet, many of us live at a level above what should be normally expected of a human being. Then, when something unexpected occurs, we are distressed and over emotional in response.

Check out these symptoms of distress. Which ones have you experienced in the last three months?

_____ increased irritability   _____ unable to get to sleep

_____ loss of appetite   _____ over eating

_____ waking up with heart   _____ feeling a sense of dread
racing   in the morning

_____ mood swings   _____ resenting others

_____ angry about little things   _____ sense of helplessness

_____ sense of unworthiness

If you are saying yes to these, you may already be at overload. It's time to take stock and slow down.

Separating Work From Home Life

You've taken a closer look at where your time goes, now let's look at those activities that crowd your time and usurp your energy. First separate work activity from home tasks. If you work outside the home:

- Leave work at work, avoid bringing work home at night.
- Do not check your work e-mail or voice mail from home.
- Teach others how to appropriately use your beeper (if you must carry one). Routine things can be communicated on voice mail, e-mail, interoffice mail and so forth. The beeper is when you are needed right away for something that requires immediate attention.
- Keep business calls at an absolute minimum at home.

The same is true at work.

- Limit personal calls.
- Pay your bills and make personal calls at home.
- Give only your home number to retail stores, libraries, church, and friends and ask that they leave a message.

You can avoid a great deal of stress by avoiding the tendency to be two people at once, and compartmentalizing your personal and business life.

If you work from home, keep work in a specified area of the house and within set hours. Otherwise you may feel that you work twenty hours a day. It is actually harder to stay organized if you work in your home, but it also has its' benefits. Breaks in your work routine may allow you to start that load of wash or get dinner in the oven. After all, your break is personal time.

One way you can visualize the activity of your busy life is to create a pie chart in the space below. Draw a circle and then divide the circle by the percentage of time you spend in any specific activity. For example, if you spend 8 hours a day at work, one-third of your circle is labeled... Work. You may see some similarities with your time use chart. After all, most of our time is used doing activities. You are likely to find there isn't enough space in the chart to place everything you do in a routine day. Bingo! That's why we are focused on simplifying life. Most women today complain of being spread too thin, but we have to stop long enough to look at where all the activity happens. Now, do the pie chart for yourself and see what you are doing all day.

Which activities can be delegated to others?

Which ones can be more organized to reduce wasted effort?

Which activities can you simply let go of?

Organizing Work Activity

In my work, I face many unscheduled problems that demand immediate attention. If this is the case for you, be sure you do not schedule every hour of the day. Allow for flexible time. Some tasks can be done at 10 a.m. or 2 p.m. Leave some time free so you can respond more effectively when these things arise. Your stress level can be reduced just by recognizing and accepting that there will be interruptions and you cannot control every event of the day.

If you work in a supervisory capacity, identify employees that have potential for further development and teach them to do some of the work that you are carrying. This does not mean to dump your unpleasant tasks onto another human being. This means to develop other people's skills, and you may become freer to take on other interesting projects yourself. Your department and the organization for whom you work are enhanced by the growth of each employee.

If you have a problem employee, address the problems. Their behavior can become a serious detriment to the organization when your good employees become frustrated by one person who does not do the job. You can lose your best staff by failing to address the one problem employee.

If you are fortunate enough to not have to work outside your home, you face another set of difficulties. You may have friends, family, community or church committee members expecting you to handle "busywork" because "you don't have to work, you can do it". You may well be an at-home mother who has made sacrifices in lifestyle so you could choose not to work and you can be with your children full time. Set your boundaries with others that don't realize being a homemaker and mother is a full time job. Your children are more important than that errand that has to be run. Seek out what has meaning to you and where you feel led to serve. Then accept that it really is okay to say no.

Even after raising a family while earning a graduate degree and working my way up the ladder, I truly believe that raising a child is the single most important job a mother has. It is a sacred trust to teach and nurture children to become productive citizens and loving parents themselves. Maybe I hold onto that belief because in my work with adolescents who have emotional and behavioral problems, I have seen so many parents that did not have the energy or ability to nurture their children. I have seen children who were desperate for attention from their parents and would do almost anything to get it, even if it meant becoming self-destructive. When our children reach their teen years, our job is not over. Adolescence is a critical developmental time in life and a teen needs parental supervision and guidance.

Organizing Home Activity

In the home, you are again faced with unanticipated demands and emergencies. Avoid scheduling every moment of your day so you will be able to respond to the needs of others. Daily tasks need to be organized. When you are consistent that naptime is at 12:30 and bedtime is 8:30, your children will learn to adapt to your framework. Develop a routine that works for your family. Now, take a look at the activities at home that involve all the various family members? What lessons and sports are your children involved in? What activities and committees or boards do you and your husband serve on? Remember your children learn by your example. While you want to teach the importance of community service, you do not want that to be at the expense of the family. Take time to list the varied activities of your family that require your time and energy.

Why are you doing each one? Is it because it is expected of you? Perhaps because you just did not want to let someone down? Is it because you felt called to serve in this way? If the answer to this last question is "No, not particularly", take a closer look. When you are busy doing good deeds, you may not be available for God to work through you as He desires.

Choose the activities that are meaningful and that fit into the purposes for which you believe you are here. Limit activity so you can do a good job of service in each one. Include one activity that you do for the sheer enjoyment.

Activities that are meaningful to me include:

Activities to let go include:

One activity I want to do for the sheer enjoyment is:

Now, teach your children to do the same. Allow them to choose a limited number of activities. Perhaps you can limit each child to one class like dance, gymnastics or piano and one or two sports per year. Your daughter may be a gifted pianist, but hates to play. If her heart is set on being a dancer, allow her to take dance instead. She may be equally talented in dance and you could just find her practicing piano on her own because she misses it. It may mean that you have to give up one of your dreams. Be sure you are not asking your child to fulfill the dream you never had a chance to live for yourself. God may not be calling your child to excel in the same thing you want him or her to do. Our children are under tremendous pressure to perform, to achieve, to excel and to compete. They can only learn how to prioritize and balance their lives if we teach them. Remember that what you do speaks louder than what you say.

Juggling family schedules can be easier if you create a family calendar and review it each week with all family members present. Look for conflicts in the schedule, when other transportation will be needed as Mom's taxi is already booked, and define what kind of help each member needs in the coming week to get things done. Consider carpooling or rotating weeks to provide transportation to sports practices. If you are exhausted running your kids around from place to place, think how tired they are of doing so much.

Types of Activity

To make room for the activities you actually enjoy, you have to clean out the undesirable activities that clutter your life. To determine any that you are chosen by God to do requires time with Him to ask for guidance before you just clutter up your life again. Another area to consider is this. Are you an extrovert or an introvert? One easy way to determine this is by answering one question. When you around other people, talking and visiting (maybe at a party), do you feel energized at the end? or drained? If being around others causes you to feel energized, you are probably an extrovert. If you work in quiet or isolation, it will be important for you to get with other people after your work day. This can be a real problem for young mothers who feel trapped at home all day. When hubby comes home tired and wants quiet, Mom can't stop talking. It isn't that he's being insensitive or you are being a chatterbox. You need an outlet. Give him some time in quiet first, then maybe he can hear you later. Schedule some time with female friends to allow the fellowship you need.

If you are drained by being around others, you are probably an introvert. You will find that you crave time alone, at peace. Quiet walks in the neighborhood while listening to the birds may be a restorative activity. Ask that your husband watch the young ones for half an hour and get off to yourself. Maybe a warm bath and a few minutes with a good novel will do the trick.

Sedentary and Active

Another balance is between sedentary and active interests. If your day is filled with lifting, carrying and moving around stuff, you may need a movie in the evening. If your work is at a desk all day, you may need a quick jog in the park. It is important to balance physical activity. When deskwork causes you to feel exhausted, get outdoors and do something physical before crashing on the couch. It will benefit both your physical and emotional health.

Again, I firmly believe that every human being needs at least one creative outlet. Try your hand at watercolors or even color in the coloring book with a young child. It really is fun, even when you're a grandma. Take a yoga class, or try pottery. Remember, the goal here is not to become an expert. The goal is to enjoy the thrill of creativity, or of learning something new. Engage in contemplative prayer, simply for the enjoyment of being in the presence of God. You were given a passion for something in life. Perhaps it is a great love of animals or nature. Perhaps you transcend the bounds of earth when attending a musical concert. God has given you the passion for nature, music, art, architecture or some other interest. The world is full of possibility, choose one thing you always wanted to do, and just do it. If you have many interests, choose one for now, do another next year. In a lifetime you can experience a great many adventures!

Chapter Four

What Am I Supposed To Do With All This Stuff?

I Timothy 6:7-8
For we brought nothing into this world, and it is certain we can carry nothing out. And having food and clothing, with these we shall be content.

Haggai 1:6
You have sown much, and bring in little; You eat, but do not have enough; you drink, but you are not filled with drink; You clothe yourselves, but no one is warm; And he that earns wages, Earns wages to put into a bag with holes.

Talk about clutter! We spend our hard-earned money on stuff to dust, stuff to pick up, stuff to wash, and stuff to pay for. All too often, we haven't earned the money to buy it yet, so we accumulate debt as well.

Isn't it amazing what our consumer economy has generated? The average eight year old today has more personal wealth in possessions than most folks from my generation had in the eighteen years we spent under our parents' roof. It is no small wonder that we are fussing at our children to pick up their room and put their things away. The saddest part of this change in consumerism is the fact that our children have much more, but appreciate it far less. Abundance is taken for granted. They are unable to identify with the meaning or experience of poverty. It is so easy for children to spend our money, but when it comes to spending their own allowance or money earned by doing yard work or babysitting, suddenly that item is less essential. Perhaps it's time for us as parents to learn a lesson from our kids. To learn the value of money, they have to experience shortage and see how far a dollar can stretch.

It Costs More Than Money

It isn't just money we spend when we buy needless items. We are also exchanging a certain amount of time...the time it takes to earn that amount of money. When you slow down and think about a purchase based on how many hours you have to work to earn it, the value becomes clearer. For instance, if you earn $10.00 an hour, you can work three hours for that pair of jeans in the department store or work six hours to earn the designer jeans. Are the expensive jeans really worth that much extra work? I handled this constant battle with my teenage daughter in this way. I would agree to pay the cost of everyday jeans. If she wanted the designer label, she could pay the difference. In adolescence when it was so important to her look and dress just right, she did pay the difference. She also took better care of her jeans. Now that she's a wife and mom, she has decided that designer clothes are not so high on the list of priorities. Learning to appreciate what we have does not just happen. We have the responsibility of teaching our children about value and priorities. This is a lesson in stewardship. Everything we have is a gift. We show appreciation by taking care of the gift.

Reasons For Spending

There's another consideration. Why do you buy a particular item? Is it because it serves a real purpose? Do you reward yourself through spending? Do you see something special and just "have" to have it? Do you spend out of boredom? Are you an emotional shopper? Are you trying to impress someone else? Take a moment and think about the purchases you have made in the last month.

Elizabeth Gregory

Which ones were bought on impulse?

Which ones did you buy with a credit card? Would you have purchased it if you had to spend cash on hand?

Did you buy any of these things because you were angry, hungry, lonely, bored or stressed?

Do you feel like you have to hide your spending from your spouse?

Sarah Ban Breathnach shares her struggle with accepting the life of both abundance and simplicity in her well-known book <u>Simple Abundance</u>. She suggests the concept that we need to clear out the clutter in our lives to allow space for abundance to fill our needs. She has a good idea to keep you from feeling overwhelmed at the idea of clearing out the household clutter. Take just one room at a time. Avoid simply moving undesirable items to another room, you will just have to move them again later.

Getting Rid of Clutter

I have to admit it, of all the steps to simplicity, getting rid of the clutter in my home, is the most difficult challenge. You know the things you tell yourself. "I might be able to wear it next year." "But my (whoever) gave this to me." The old adage that if you haven't used it or worn it in a year, it's time to let it go is pretty good advice here. My problem is not that I'm a packrat. I'm incredibly sentimental. I pick up something to throw away and the memory of when I bought it, or the person who gave it to me comes flooding back. Face it. Some things are too precious to throw away. Instead of packing them off to the basement, see how they can be used or displayed. Make space for them in your life today. Perhaps that item would be appreciated by another family member or close friend. Pass it along! Then you can continue to enjoy it when you visit them.

Think about what keeps you from throwing out the things that clutter your life. Could it be that you are afraid of the emptiness that will be left if you throw things out? There is a term used by artists. Instead of a space being empty, it is negative space. That negative space creates a balance and allows the items in the painting to be more appreciated. It could be that your buying items to fill up space is an attempt to fill some other void in your life. Could you be buying everything for yourself or others now to make up for what you lacked in your childhood? It may actually be an emptiness that cannot be filled with things. It isn't things that really add meaning to our lives. Sarah Ban Breathnach suggests, "When we choose not to focus on what is missing from our lives but on the abundance that's present—love, health, family, friends, work, and personal pursuits that bring us pleasure—the wasteland falls away and we experience joy in the real lives we live each day". Again, like the negative space in a painting, having less allows us to appreciate what we have even more.

As you clean out, remember there are many others who have real need for your extras. Contact local community agencies and missions. Consider donating anything others can use. It was a ritual in our home to clean out prior to Christmas. The children could pull out toys that didn't suit them or were now too babyish and pass these on to Goodwill or Salvation Army. Then it was time to pick one item each child would like to receive for Christmas, and buy that item for Toys For Tots in our community. This teaches so many valuable lessons. A child learns when it is time to let go of extra stuff, when to give to others and not just to give away discards, but to also give of our best.

We can outgrow things by growing up, or out at my age, and by becoming a different person who has changed desires and styles. The dresses you wore three years ago may not fit the personality of the woman you have become since then. Through seeking simplicity, you may find the desires of the past lose their power over you and you can accept a much simpler life as one of abundance. What was it that Paul told us? In Philippians 4:11 he says, "...for I have learned, in whatever state I am, therewith to be content." This is a worthwhile goal to strive for.

E-Rage

In our modern day society, we have another type of clutter that women never had to deal with before. We have the new, improved, expensive and constantly changing electronic devices! We coined a new phrase where I work when my employer changed out all the computer systems and replaced them with a new server. You may know the frustration of getting the hang of a system, just to have it taken away so you can learn all over again. We call it e-rage! The name caught on so fast, I was asked to do radio talk shows, television spots and a newspaper interview on e-rage. Let me explain further.

Most of us can easily recall a time when we have experienced a moment of anger at one of the many machines we are forced to use in our modern society. Automatic teller machines led the way to a technological age that forces us to learn how to use a wide variety of machines in our daily work and life. Where does e-rage come from? One of the leading causes is the telephone. There's nothing new about the phone, we've been using that a long time! No, it's not the phone itself that causes the rage. It's the phone menus used by so many businesses now that irks us as we listen to a menu, pick a number, go through another menu, pick a number and then get put on hold because all the customer service representatives are busy. You know the old "Please hold on, your call will be answered in the order it was received". Do you ever want to throw the phone across the room and yell "where are all the people?" Then, you, my friend, have experienced e-rage.

Another primary cause is the computer. This is not surprising. Many of us are expected to use a computer in our work although we have never received any formal training for how this contraption operates. Have you ever seen that cute little screen that says, "you have committed an illegal act"? Now why use the term illegal? Why not, "you have made an error, allow me to show you how to correct it." No, you committed an illegal act and the computer police are sure to come along any minute to take you away. Do you suppose they have developed a torture device that outdoes the computer?

E-mail is another area for frustration. HAVE YOU EVER RECEIVED AN E-MAIL THAT IS ALL IN CAPITAL LETTERS? DON'T YOU FEEL LIKE YOU ARE BEING YELLED AT? It's simply a matter of the capital button being pushed on the sender's keyboard, but it sure can be annoying. That's the basic problem with e-mail. All you get is the words. You do not get voice tone, pitch, or volume. You do not get facial expressions or gestures. You do not get the chance to say, "stop a minute, I need you to clarify that last statement." Body language adds a lot to our communication and it is totally missing in e-mail.

Then there's voice mail. When calling someone, do you get those messages that say "If you need to reach me immediately, you can page me at...". Why would I call if I had not intended to talk to you now? Even worse is the fact that you have gotten so used to never catching anyone in their office or at home, that you expect to get the message and are surprised when a live voice answers.

Elizabeth Gregory

Another technology that has gotten completely out of hand is the pager. Everybody has a pager. Are we really so important that the world cannot survive if we are out of touch long enough to drive to work or to the grocery store? It used to be a status symbol. Only doctors carried a pager. Now it's just another nuisance. From pagers, we went to cell phones...and pagers that are cell phones. Are these necessary? Yes, if you are a health care professional on call for an emergency. But does your teenager need one of these? I hate it when I receive a page at 2:30 in the morning. I wake up with adrenaline flowing and am ready to respond to an emergency. Instead, when I return the call, I get some kid on the line who dialed a wrong number!

What of cell phone etiquette? Is it rude to carry on a conversation on the cell phone when you are having lunch with someone? Is it now acceptable to carry on private conversations in public places and expect everyone around you to just pretend they don't hear? Don't you hate it when the person next to you has a cell phone ringing? Not only do they answer it, they continue to carry on a conversation. Are they really oblivious to the fact that they are distracting others? I encourage you to assert yourself when you are in a meeting, lecture or movie and you have a thoughtless cell phone addict sitting next to you. This behavior reminds me of the days when cigarette smokers filied the theatre lobbies and public restrooms. They too were oblivious to know how annoying they were to others.

Enough already! What can we do to combat e-rage? First off, remember, you can turn off the machine. You can hang up the phone that has a ridiculous number of choices on the never-ending menus. Many of these menu selections will end and you will be forwarded to a human if you touch the "O". Write that company and tell the management how annoying their telephone menu is and that you as a customer want to talk to a real live person who can actually answer your questions. Remember also, you are dealing with a machine. It will not respond to your emotions. Be aware of the increasing frustration as you work with the machinery and give yourself a periodic break. Set some boundaries. Avoid checking your office e-mail and voice mail from home. Be at home and focus on your family for a while! And finally, be honest with yourself. Do you really need all the latest technology in your home? Do you need that pager, cell phone, fax machine? Maybe what you need most of all is a little peace and quiet.

Putting all this together and actually clearing out the clutter of material possessions is a difficult task. Don't overwhelm yourself by setting a goal to get it done next weekend. Set a reasonable time frame, maybe as long as a year, and go about it one step at a time. At the end, you will find that life is simpler. Then, as in all steps to simplicity, avoid repeating old habits. Before buying any item, ask yourself, "What is the purpose of this item, why am I buying it, and is it worth exchanging the amount of time required to earn it?".

Chapter Five

How Can Managing My Money Simplify My Life?

Acts 8:20-21
But Peter said to him, Your money perish with you, because you thought that the gift of God could be purchased with money. You have neither part nor portion in this matter, for your heart is not right in the sight of God.

How do you use your money? Is it to further the kingdom of God, or used to impress others? Allow me to strongly recommend a book first released in 1992 by Dave Ramsey. The title is <u>Financial Peace</u> and in this book, Dave tells his own story of the struggle with using money unwisely and accumulating debt. He shares wonderful insights and ideas that can transform the way you look at money. His book and radio program to which I listened with great regularity was my answer to prayer in finding a way out of debt that threatened to drown me following a divorce. Even following Dave's advice, it took me over seven years to reach a point that my only remaining debt was a mortgage. The long struggle taught me to manage money more wisely. Being able to afford the

51

payment on something is not the same as being able to afford the item. One of Dave's best suggestions is to perform "plastic surgery". He is referring to the plastic credit cards that have made it so easy for us to sell our souls to the creditors. Cutting up these cards is a huge step toward your own emancipation. Proverbs 22:7 tells us that the borrower is servant to the lender. Have you ever owed so much money that you felt imprisoned by your debt? Have you ever been afraid to make a change in your life because your debts were too high and prevented you from being able to afford making a desirable change? You cannot pay off debt until you stop creating it. Dave also offers excellent advice on paying off debt using the "snowball" technique. Let me give you an idea how this works. Let's say Joan starts out owing the following:

	Monthly payment	Total owed
Department store card 1	30.00	320.00
Department Store card 2	25.00	200.00
Car	325.00	9000.00
Furniture loan	125.00	1250.00
Totals	$ 505.00	$10770.00

Joan should start out paying off the lowest debt first, while she continues paying the minimum payment on all other debts. So she pays the $25.00 plus enough to reduce the rate of incurring interest (let's say $40.00) to store 2 for eight months or so. When she pays off store 2, she applies the $40.00 she was paying them to her $30.00 payment to store 1. Now she is paying $70.00 a month to store 1 until it is paid off. Then she adds the $70.00 payment to the $125.00 going to the furniture loan until it is paid off. You can see that this will be paid off much faster when she applies all she can instead of just paying the minimum. When the furniture is paid off, she can knock out that car loan by paying out $450.00 a month!

You see how the amount snowballs. Be honest now. You know as well as I do that once you pay off store 2, you tend to keep paying the minimum to all the others and paying enormous amounts of interest unnecessarily. What keeps you from following Dave's advice? I can tell you my excuses. "I have to keep a credit card for emergencies." Not true, that's why you set up enough in savings to take care of those things before you start paying off debts. "But I never know when my children are going to need something for a special event", you say. Guess what. Your children need to learn to live within your means too.

If you overspend, stop going to the shopping malls and throw out catalogues. The visual stimulation is designed to make you desire things you do not really need. The whole idea is to convince you to spend money. The reality is that we do not want to accept that we all have financial limits. Learning to live within our means is a tough experience. You do need to focus on the abundance in your life instead of all the other things you want. You do have to accept that our worth as children of God is not measured by our material possessions.

How do you know if you are in financial trouble?

Here are the warning signs. Check the ones that have applied to you during the last twelve months.

_____ Credit cards at the maximum limit

_____ Getting another credit card to pay off the first one

_____ Buying items based on the monthly charge rather than actual cost of the item.

_____ Juggling bills so that the same ones will not be late every month.

_____ Not saving money every month

_____ Having no money to come close to tithing

_____ Having no money to assist in worthwhile charities

_____ Impulse shopping or compulsive spending

_____ Receiving late notices on bills

_____ Receiving calls from creditors due to lateness of payment

_____ Borrowing money for routine expenses

_____ Using cash advance scams

_____ Using title loan business to borrow against your paid off car

_____ Borrowing against your mortgage (equity loans)

_____ Using rent to own because you can't get credit to buy

_____ Working another job to get you by (and being away from family because of the debt)

_____ Considering bankruptcy

American Debt Patterns

If you are an average American consumer, you have probably checked several of these danger signals. Debtsavers analyzes consumer spending information released by the Federal Reserve and they report that at the end of 1999 over 78 million households now have at least one credit card with the average credit card debt reaching $7,564. Even with all the low interest marketing done by credit card companies, the average weighted interest rate is still over 18%. At the end of 1999, Americans have "racked up $462 billion in bank card debt and another $88 billion in retail store debt". We talk about a booming economy, yet family debt has increased over 42% since 1995. Just in the last year, Americans have charged more than $400 billion in credit cards and are paying an additional $50 billion in interest. One of the saddest trends is the tremendous increase of debt in low-income families. According to Debtsavers, "It's common to see families that make $25,000 or less that have run up to $35,000 or more in credit card debts". This is nothing short of insane behavior on the part of average American citizens! It is time to take back control of our finances and learn to live within our means. Credit card companies are not doing you a favor, they are getting rich off your lack of control. There are now many good consumer credit counseling programs to help you. Some of these groups have relationships with creditors and can get late charges waived and help consolidate all debt to one payment. Then, you have to make an agreement that you will incur no further debt while using their service. Be sure to check out their reputation in your community and perhaps with your Better Business Bureau. You can reach Debtsavers at www.debtfree.org or call (954) 484-3328.

Stewardship

It is imperative to have a workable system to keep track of your bills and payment record. I found it useful to keep a ledger book with each month's bills and due dates. I checked off each payment as it was made, then highlighted each one that was paid off in full that month. The highlighted one was then not carried over to the next month. I cannot express the exhilaration I felt when I could use that marker and my list for the next month got shorter! I strongly encourage couples to pay the bills and balance the checkbook together. Finances seem to be the most intimate part of a relationship, even more than the sexual intimacy we share with our spouse. You will learn an immense amount about your values and learn to manage conflict as you develop a system to manage your finances.

If we change our view of money from something we earn and deserve to an awareness that every dime is a gift from God, we may develop a new sensitivity on spending wisely. Yes, you worked long hours to earn every penny. Who gave you the mind to reason, a healthy body, an ability to organize the work and be successful in your endeavors? Do I even need to answer that one? If God gave us the ability to earn our wage, then he also deserves the credit for anything we accomplish...and we should be using that money in a way that is pleasing to him. We are only the stewards of His gifts. The next point we tend to ignore is that the more He blessed us, the more He expects from us. Prayer is vital in establishing a relationship with God that allows us to even talk over money matters with Him. He is not just interested in our spirituality. He wants to be involved in every sphere in our lives. So, as you plan a budget and approach the task of getting out of debt, seek God's advice.

Another area that needs to be seriously thought out is that of charities you feel led to support. If you and your spouse prayerfully consider the needs of your church and the many other mission oriented organizations around you, which needs speak to your heart? Which ones stand for something you believe in and are willing to invest in? Include these donations and tithe in your budget. This will give you the courage to tell phone solicitors that you have made decisions about organizations you will support, and therefore cannot contribute to their cause. If you want to consider them further, ask that they send you information in the mail and you will consider placing them on the list if you feel led to do so at a later time.

Club memberships need the same kind of review.

There are many worthwhile items to be bought at discounts through club memberships. Music, books, even coffee and tea are but a few of these. However, it is much easier to fill out a card when the monthly newsletter arrives and pay later. You may be spending more than you would if you had to go to the trouble to look for what you actually need. Magazine and newspaper subscriptions are also worth a quick review. Do you really read all of them? If not, let go of some of the clutter being mailed into your home at your request. To get rid of all that extra stuff you receive in the mail, you can request to be taken off junk mail lists. You can also reduce the phone calls that interrupt your family time at home.

Write to the   Mail Preference Service
Direct Marketing Association
P.O. Box 9008
Farmingdale, NY 11735-9008

and to the   Telephone Preference Service
Direct Mailing Association
P.O. Box 9014
Farmingdale, NY 11735-9008

Teaching Children the Value of Money

Now let's look at our spending pattern and what that teaches our children about the value of money. There is a lot of debate over the concept of paying children an allowance for doing their share of the work in the family home. After all, it's their home too. Shouldn't they be expected to help take care of things? Do I have to pay them to pick up their own toys? Certainly not! But, it is up to the parents to teach two things here. One is how to wisely use money. The other is to do their share as a member of a family. Some parents use these daily and weekly chores as a means to an end. If they are paid for chores, then they suffer if they do not do their work. It's the same principle as adults earning a wage at work. Do we do the work well because we get paid for it, or because it's the right thing to do? After all, aren't we supposed to do every task as though it were unto the Lord?

Some parents combat this confusing issue by separating allowance from the chores they believe a child should be doing just because the family shares in the work to help each other. Allowances are just a set sum given to each child weekly to take care of their personal needs; lunches at school, paper and pens, snacks, drinks, gifts for others and so forth. The child is taught to budget. For example, a teenager is given $15.00 a week; $1.50 is for tithing, $7.50 is used for school lunch. An additional 60 cents a day is spent on a soft drink (soda if you're from up north), and $1.00 for school supplies. That leaves $2.00 a week to save for gifts, extra desires and so forth. Then chores are related to earning privileges and rewards other than money. For instance, if Joe does not clean his room, he does not get to go to friend's house to play later. If homework is not done, then he cannot talk on the phone that evening until he has completed his work.

As you can see, money is really a loaded issue! We all receive countless messages to spend more, to have more and to give more of our limited resources. Money supplies our basic necessities and helps fulfill many of our desires. It is worth taking the time to think seriously about what money means to you and how it is used in your family. By taking the time to talk through this issue and budgeting ahead, communication in the family can improve and fights over the lack of money can be reduced, or maybe even eliminated.

Chapter Six

How On Earth Do You Simplify Relationships?

I Corinthians 13:3-7
And though I bestow all my goods to feed the poor, and though I give my body to be burned, but have not love, it profits me nothing. Love suffers long and is kind; love does not envy; love does not parade itself, is not puffed up; does not behave rudely, does not seek its own, is not provoked, thinks no evil; does not rejoice in iniquity, but rejoices in the truth; bears all things, believs all things, hopes all things, endures all things.

The seasons and times of our lives take us through an amazing variety of relationships. One thing I want to suggest is to accept and appreciate each relationship in the season for which it was intended. Some friendships last a lifetime and become increasingly more meaningful with time. Others may last only a season, whether that be a few days, weeks or months, but are no less valuable because of their limited time. God may have brought this person into your life for a specific purpose and once that purpose was served, allowed them to quietly slip away. Yet that person's influence may last a lifetime.

One such person for me was a neighbor, Juanita. I treasure all she shared with me and have loved her through my whole life. I tried to locate her when I was grown and was unable to find her, so I have never had the opportunity to let her know what a powerful impact she had on my ability to appreciate nature, hiking, and birds. It was because of her that I have supported the Audubon Society and conservation societies. She took me, a child of ten, with her to Audubon events and other environmental outings. She showed me how to care for injured wild animals. I have a stronger understanding of the relationship between humankind and nature to this day, thirty something years later. My husband and I now enjoy the birds on our seven feeders and even the occasional mischievous squirrel and raccoon who also want a bite to eat.

We can all have an impact on the lives of others by introducing them to new activities. Consider introducing a child to a wider life experience by taking them to a museum, a concert, a ballet, or horseback riding. Allow a child to watch you paint a flower arrangement in watercolor. Simply reading stories to a child may stir a life long love of reading or create a future writer. Children are enriched when they are allowed to see the wide expanse of interests and activities available to them. You may have a child living next door who is a budding artist, but has no one in their family who enjoys artistic pursuits. You may be the link God put in place to awaken the artistic spirit within. A child on your son's baseball team may be a future minister, yet lives in a family that does attend church. Without your invitation, that child may miss his calling. We can have a major impact on young lives without even realizing it. I'm sure Juanita never intended to touch me as deeply as she did.

The primary relationships we have in our lives include our family of origin (parents and siblings), immediate family (spouse and children), extended family, church family, community, work colleagues, and friends. The most important of relationships is the one with our creator. Developing a closer relationship with our Heavenly Father requires a chapter of it's own. We will look at this later.

Family of Origin

Our relationships with parents and siblings change through the seasons of our lives. We start out being totally dependent on our parents for our physical needs as well as emotional nurturance and mental development. As children, our first understanding of who we are comes from these important people. When as a child, we receive the message that we are lovable, worthy of affection and hold the promise for a wonderful life, we enter life with anticipation and joy. Every daily event can become a magical moment to the child raised with encouragement. If our parents lack the understanding of a child's needs and fail to nurture and encourage our growth, we may be anxious about daily events and feel we cannot handle simple tasks.

Siblings can also be encouraging or destructive in a child's development. Negativity, sarcasm, and criticism can stunt the emotional growth of a sensitive child just as surely as lack of nutritious food and water can stunt physical growth. You are indeed fortunate if you were blessed with a loving and nurturing family.

If your parents were unable or unwilling to encourage your growth, perhaps God brought others into your life that recognized your unique potential. There were two others that had a strong influence in my life, just because they loved me. One is affectionately called Mom Tully. She is my best friend's mother and had six children of her own. Yet she always made me feel like a part of the family. My friend, Helen is closer to me than any family member. She is the one person who knows the whole truth about me, but loves me anyway. Her Mom was always ready to take us swimming and to watch us play. She fixed lunches of spam sandwiches and huge servings of love. The other was "Father John", a chaplain and the director of the nurses' chorus where I attended nursing school. He provided fathering for me at a time that I needed emotional support. Because of his encouragement, I have spent a lifetime singing to the glory of God and coming closer to my heavenly Father through music. Both of these parental figures made lasting impressions on me. I have no doubt that God had a hand in leading me to them.

There are, unfortunately, far too many children, who did not receive the necessary components for development of a healthy love of self. If we do not learn to love ourselves through the love of parents or other parental figures, we are unable to extend love to others. Did you have "Godsends" in your life that loved you and helped to nurture you? Have you ever let them know how much they have meant to you? Name them here and make a comment about the gifts you received from each one.

A healthy sense of love and respect for ourselves is imperative to enable us to form healthy relationships, seek a mate with whom we are equally yoked or nurture our own children. For some individuals in our self-absorbed society, the first honest relationship they will ever experience is with a professional therapist. After more than twenty years in the mental health field, it still breaks my heart to have adolescents and even adults enter treatment because they have never received unconditional love or encouragement. For many, their parents allowed continual abuse to occur in the home and they have never known safety or security. As society has picked up the pace of life causing us to run faster and faster, we have forgotten the imperative need of intimacy. Our society has moved from front porches, to back decks and fenced yards. We have closed ourselves in air conditioned homes, and are being entertained by television and electronics instead of interaction with other humans. We drive in an increasing hurry to get somewhere to do something that is, of course, terribly important and now suffer from the lack of exercise we used to get by walking to school or to town. Modern conveniences have certainly improved our ability to utilize free time, but at what cost to individuals?

The Impact of Divorce

The divorce rate in America has drastically increased since my childhood. I should know, I'm in those statistics myself.

Although the divorce rate reportedly hit its peak in 1985, we still experience over one million divorces each year in this country. You may not agree, but I do believe there are some marriages that need to end: those where family members are abused, where alcoholism and addictions have damaged the relationship beyond repair or where extramarital affairs have destroyed any hope of regaining intimacy. But many marriages end because of the inability of emotionally starved adults to extend love, compassion and forgiveness to one another.

Most divorces occur in the first ten years of marriage, where there are young children involved and as these rates have climbed, more children are raised in poverty and left alone to seek outside their family for love, acceptance and a sense of belonging. We now see the increasing trend of gang involvement. The gang becomes a family that defends and protects its' members from outsiders and that gives a kid a sense of identity. When this occurs, the family failed. The church and community have failed this family as well. Rather than blame the parent, we as a society need to address the needs of overwhelmed and over extended families. I know how hard it is to work all day, take care of a house and yard, meet the needs of children and have any time or energy left for self growth. When a single mother is running on empty, she has little to offer her children. I am not saying here that if a child comes from a single parent home, he or she is condemned to a miserable or unsuccessful life. I always resented the referrals to "broken homes" in the years I struggled to provide a safe, secure and loving home for my daughter. Yet the reality is that being single parent is not the easiest way to raise a child.

With the increased mobility of individuals throughout our country, and even abroad, many of us lack the support of an extended family. Children rarely remain in their hometowns. Few grandparents are available to help with raising children due to geographical distances or working long hours themselves. Parents do not have the guidance in teaching children that they could easily receive when Mom lived down the street.

Single Parenting

In healthy marriages, both partners share the responsibility of providing for their children's needs. When one parent is tired of being the bad guy, they can swap off roles and let the other be the disciplinarian for a while. As a parent, you may be great with babies and toddlers, but quickly lose your patience with a ten year old. Your spouse may be able to relate much better to an older child, so you can balance each other's strengths and weaknesses. In a single parent home, there is no one to relieve the weary parent.

Friendships and church support are more important now than at any point in the past. Yet single moms often lose friends in the divorce process when women distance from them as though divorce is contagious, and they seem to believe that the now single woman is going to be a bad influence or go after her husband. Our churches do not know how to minister to single adults. It is not that churches are anti-single. They just tend to focus on the needs of the family. A divorced parent does not fit into a class for singles or for young married couples. The older single classes are often filled with widowed persons who do not understand the effects of divorce. Single parents want to be involved in the church to assure that their children receive the religious training that is so vital to manage in today's world.

I was not so aware of any discrimination as a single parent, although there was not a class in which I felt comfortable. When I remarried, however, it was as if I had attained some prestigious status. Suddenly, people were friendlier and my comments were treated as more important. In my upbringing, I was taught that to be successful as a woman meant I must have a successful husband. I never believed that teaching until I experienced the sudden elevation in respect I received when I remarried. This may well be a southern phenomenon and could differ in various regions. I am only suggesting that if you are uncomfortable with divorced people or single parents, you need to take a closer look at how you interact with them and how your church can meet their needs for acceptance, love and support.

Healthy Families

In the traditional family of two loving parents, our children have the opportunity to observe role models of healthy behavior. They can watch their parents handle disagreements in a constructive manner, exhibit respect to each other and share in daily responsibilities. By sharing the workload, each parent has more energy to focus attention on the children. Healthy and emotionally balanced families can prepare children to handle almost anything life brings their way. The children learn to trust others, allow others to help them, extend themselves to help others and communicate effectively. With these skills, they have a head start in life. When a firm foundation and belief system are formed within the family, the child has numerous resources on which to draw when life's problems arise. In his book, The 7 Habits of Highly Effective Families, Stephen Covey recommends that families develop a mission statement. This forces you, as a family, to seriously consider what the family unit means and what you have to offer to each member of the family. He states, "For the most part, families don't have the kind of mission statement so critical to organizational success. Yet the family is the most important, fundamental organization in the world". The family is the basic unit of society and from it flows the values of the entire culture. We cannot blame teachers, school officials or politicians for the declining values in society. We cannot even lay the blame on the media. It is within the family that the child learns the basic principles of honesty, trust, integrity and compassion. The parents are charged with the responsibility to supervise the child's activities, including television time, music purchases, internet access and peer involvement. Our responsibility as a society is to support the parents in this role.

The Role of Friendships

Healthy families can allow family members to maintain friendships outside of the family. Women need other female friends, men need male friends and children need friendships with other children. In marriage relationships that are mature and secure, even a friend of the opposite gender is no real threat to the integrity of the marriage. However, if either partner in the marriage is threatened by a friend of the opposite sex, the marriage relationship must come first. Friendships also go through seasons. I have one lifelong friend. Helen and I grew up as neighbors and best friends. She knows me better than any family member. My daughter views her as another aunt. We even lost a period of about five years due to a misunderstanding and miscommunication. It took one of us reaching out to mend the gap. We managed to get to the core issue several years later when she finally revealed to me why she had stopped communication with me. I had to muster up the courage to ask. Then we could forgive, forget and move on to a deeper friendship. The friendships in a woman's life may take many forms as we shift through the seasons of mothering, nurturing, supporting and playing. I do not know if men experience the same level of emotional intimacy that women often do. The way we share our deepest thoughts, dreams and concerns with one another is powerful indeed. If you do not have at least one long-term close friend, you are missing a real treasure.

Step-Parenting

If you have married into a family and become a step-parent, it is so important that you avoid trying to replace the child's biological parent. Even the child may delve into a fantasy of the perfectly normal two-parent family and want to avoid the other parent. Be sure to speak of the parent with respect and understanding. Allow the child to keep a picture of Mom or Dad by the bedside. Our role as step-parents is more like the role of an aunt. We set limits, exact consequences for misbehavior, support, offer encouragement and deeply love the child. But, we will never be the true parent. There are some biological parents that will not stay in touch with their child, yet the child will likely have an innate longing to know them. They may aggrandize them and create an unrealistic image of the parent. Present reality to the child, yet avoid branding the missing parent as a failure and not worthy of the child's caring. Remember, a part of that parent lives within the child. If you paint the other parent as all bad, the child may fear that they are just like them and you will not love them either.

Second marriages actually end in divorce more often than first ones do and arguments over the children from the first marriage are a major cause of discontent. If you are the custodial parent, realize that your second spouse did not know your child from birth, did not form the bond with him or her as an infant and may not understand your child's behaviors. It is only natural as a step-parent to be a bit less open and a bit more critical. The step-parent can help you see your child as others see him or her. This can give you valuable information when you do not want to see the negative or unhealthy behaviors your child may exhibit. In divorce and remarriage situations, acceptance and forgiveness are essential. If one parent remains critical, judgmental, angry and accusatory toward the other parent, the child cannot maintain the healthy bond needed with both parents. Divorce is a true test of one's values, faith and maturity.

Marriage

Now, for the most important relationship, the one with our marriage partner. The Bible has given us guidelines for this, but it has often been misquoted to include only the woman's responsibility. We frequently hear the part, "*Wives, submit to your own husbands as to the Lord. For the husband is the head of the wife, as also Christ is the head of the church: and He is the Savior of the body. Therefore, just as the church is subject to Christ, so let the wives be to their own husbands in everything.*" (Ephesians 5:22-24) Now telling wives to submit to their husbands in all things is anathema to our society today. We are taught by society to be independent, able to think for ourselves and to take care of ourselves. How dare we think about submitting to the authority of the husband! Stay with me here. We must also consider the husband's part in caring for the wife. "*Husbands, love your wives, just as Christ also loved the church and gave Himself for it, that He might sanctify and cleanse it with the washing of water by the word, that He might present it to Himself a glorious church, not having spot or wrinkle or any such thing, but that it should be holy and without blemish. So husbands ought to love their own wives as their own bodies. He who loves his wife loves himself. For no man ever hated his own flesh; but nourishes and cherishes it, just as the Lord does the church.*" (Ephesians 5:25-29) This paints a very different picture indeed. It is one thing to submit to, trust and honor a man who follows the commands of God to love you as his own flesh, to nourish you and cherish you and be willing to give his very life to save you.

Such a marriage can be enormously satisfying and enriching. With such a partner in life, we are free to continue growing. When you rely on God to choose your life partner, this is the kind of man He desires for you. A marriage based on God's leadership and committed to following God's plan is a rewarding experience. We can accomplish great things through the strength of God's love. This marriage can withstand storms, adversity and temptations.

It is a different thing altogether to submit yourself to a man who beats you, ridicules you, tears you down emotionally and is incapable of loving you. Even worse is trapping children in this kind of abuse. Is God commanding that you submit to abuse? I don't think so. Staying in such a relationship is detrimental to the entire family. If you are in such a destructive marriage, please enter with God prayerfully to seek His will in your life. Man may call you to hear only the part of the scripture that tells wives to submit, while God may be calling you to a life of peace. Divorce cannot be taken lightly, but you are to revere your body as the temple of the Lord and I do not believe that means allowing someone to destroy you. Richard Foster in his 1978 book Celebration of Discipline had this to say about submission. "The limits of the Discipline of submission are at the points at which it becomes destructive. It then becomes a denial of the law of love as taught by Jesus and is an affront to biblical submission."

The marriage relationship described by Paul in Ephesians even rings of peace and love as you read it. When a couple places God in the center of the relationship and He is head of the family, He will direct the husband to wise decisions and fair treatment of every member of his household. It is easy to submit to such a man because he is deserving of your trust and respect. Respect and trust are basic elements in a healthy marriage. If they are lacking in your relationship, do not ignore the warning signs. Seek guidance from other successful and happy couples, your church family and leaders, professional counselors and in prayer. Share with your husband the desire you have for a deeper, more committed relationship with Christ as a couple. God will enrich you individually and as a couple. Your children will benefit beyond measure.

Relationships That Clutter Your Life

Relationships are the most complex part of our lives. I urge you not to hold onto relationships that actually clutter your life and force you to expend unnecessary energy. Do you have a friend who causes you to feel exhausted and weary every time you talk with her? Do you find yourself avoiding her? This may well be a relationship that you do not need to continue. If a relationship causes you to feel off balance, down on yourself and leaves you doubting yourself, or leads you to unhealthy behaviors, you must stop and consider, "Do I really need this relationship in my life?". If you are wasting energy trying to rescue a friend that obviously has no desire to use any of your advice, then it may be time to break the bond, suggest they seek professional help and move on. Find healthier relationships that help motivate you, encourage you to grow and strengthen your faith.

Review

Take a few minutes now to evaluate the key relationships in your life:

Did you receive love and encouragement from your parents?

Were there other parental figures in your life that encouraged your growth?

Do you have a close intimate friendship with a female friend?

Does your husband have any close male friends?

Do your children feel free to form friendships outside of the family and to invite friends into your home?

Is God in the center of your marriage relationship?

Are you harboring bitterness or resentments toward your spouse? How long has this been going on?

Are you living in a destructive marriage?

Relationships are the essence of life. We all need others to love and respect us. We all need someone who will alert us when we are fooling ourselves and moving toward tragic mistakes. Are you also a good friend to others? Are you trustworthy in your relationships? If you are finding that your relationships are not fulfilling your needs, allow yourself to search out the answers about the changes you need to make. Do not act hastily to make any major changes. Seek the counsel of others you trust as you evaluate life decisions.

I mentioned the unique bonds we, as women experience in our relationships. The following meditation expresses a part of what I was referring to.

Reflections

A mother is a nurturing woman,
one sensitive to the needs of our very souls.
She responds to the needs of the body
with food and drink,
maybe even Spam sandwiches
on bread spread with Miracle Whip.
She responds to our need for physical activity
and for rest,
watching us play on a hot summer day
and calling us into the house to catch our breath.
To be a mother,
one does not necessarily give physical birth to the child.
She adopts the child as one of her own
and simply shares her love.

I was blessed to witness the early moments
of motherhood
following the birth of my grandson.
As I watched my daughter gaze into the eyes
of her newborn son,
her eyes filled with tears
of joy and a tender love
she had never before experienced.
Unknown to her, her husband gazed at her,
his eyes also filled with the tears
of love and gratitude.
I knew at that moment
that she was loved
and the two of them
will share the journey of life
together.

A daughter
is one who cherishes a woman
with whom she feels a soul connection.
The mother we love may be our own or someone else's.
She may be old enough to be our mother,
or of our own age.
She may be our mother this moment
and in a flash,
transform
into our sister
and friend.

Friend,
what a commonly used word,
but a rare connection.
A true friend
is an integral part of ourselves.
One who has seen all the flaws and defects.
One who has witnessed
failures and struggles
in our mundane lives.
One who kept our secrets.
One who loves us
in spite of all she has seen.
A friend is a sister
of the spirit,
allowing us to soar
above the trials of life.
A friend is a rare treasure.

These intimate relationships
unique to women,
how blessed we are
to experience each expression of love
pure and unselfish.

I offer my gratitude
to those who are my mother,
my daughter,
my sister,
and my friend.
I cannot imagine
a life devoid of your inspiration.
God richly blessed my life
when He allowed me
to share my days with you.

Elizabeth C. Gregory
Mother's Day, 1999

Chapter Seven

Taking Care of You: A Step Toward Simplifying Your Life

I Corinthians 6:19-20
Or do you not know that your body is the temple of the Holy Spirit who is in you, whom you have from God, and you are not your own? For you were bought at a price; therefore glorify God in your body and in your spirit, which are God's.

Women often are so concerned with taking care of others, that we fail to care for ourselves. Many women are unaware of the health risks we face. We have difficulty following the basics of eating a balanced diet, getting adequate sleep and exercising regularly. Yet, it is our example that teaches our children how to care for their health. If we teach unhealthy patterns, we have set them up to fight these patterns when they reach adulthood. If we are sick or die, who is going to raise our children for us? Taking care of your health is important. Your body is the temple of God if His spirit lives in you. God's temple is certainly worthy of your care.

Women and Heart Disease

Sara Jenkins was a busy single Mom. She managed a full time job and three children with little outside help. She felt the daily pressures of getting everyone where they needed to go and rarely took the time to properly care for herself. Fast food was the easiest way to fit eating into her crowded schedule and exercise consisted of running after her two pre-school children each night. The end of the day found Sara exhausted and often too wound up to get to sleep. Sometimes she even carried work home with her to complete after the children were in bed.

A typical Tuesday started just like any other. Sara had been feeling nauseous early in the morning. Later, her chest felt heavy. "The workload is getting to me," she thought. As the day progressed, she felt worse and finally decided she must be coming down with a virus. At the insistence of her co-workers, she went to see her physician. He seemed very concerned. He ordered an EKG to be done in the office, then drew labwork. The physician started asking questions about the history of heart disease in Sara's family. "Why are you asking me about this?" Sara asked. "I'm concerned you may have had a mild heart attack", he responded. "But that's impossible, women don't have heart attacks!, she exclaimed.

85

Sara, like most women assumed that heart disease generally affects only men. However, nearly 500,000 women die of heart attacks each year. You may know the classic symptoms in men: crushing pain in the chest, possibly radiating to the jaw or arm, shortness of breath, and nausea. Women often do not present that typical picture, but have milder symptoms like Sara's that are easily ignored and seen as just the effects of stress. Women are more likely to complain of fatigue, nausea, sometimes dizziness and confusion, shortness of breath and difficulty breathing, unexplained anxiety, weakness, and cold sweats. The pain is likely to be in the abdominal region rather than in the chest. This leads to a tendency to write off the symptoms as a virus. What is even worse is the fact that women are almost twice as likely than men to die during the first year after a heart attack.

Are you at high risk? Here are the primary risk factors:

- Post menopausal
- family history of heart disease
- high blood pressure
- high cholesterol
- obesity (over 20 pounds overweight)
- sedentary lifestyle
- diabetes

- smoking
- race (more common in African-American women)

Let's take a closer look at what causes heart disease and then address the risk factors. Every time your heart beats, it sends oxygen rich blood through the arteries to all parts of the body. Coronary Artery Disease develops as the blood vessels that lead back to the heart become clogged with a fatty substance called cholesterol or plaque. As these build up in the vessel, more pressure is required to force the circulation of blood through them and the work of the heart muscle is increased. The arteries become stiff or hardened, a condition called atheroschlerosis. When the heart muscle cannot get the oxygen it needs because of the clogging in the vessels, you may experience pain called angina. Angina is actually a warning signal. If a woman is not checking her blood pressure or cholesterol to allow her early warning, she may have a heart attack before she is aware she has heart disease.

According to the American Heart Association in 1999, there were 17,346 deaths in Alabama that were related to heart disease. Of those deaths, 9074 were women and 8272 were men. One third of these were from the Jefferson county area alone. It is important for women to recognize that heart disease does affect them and to take measures to reduce their risk. "Because heart disease does not start to affect women in the mid-life period when men are first diagnosed, women often have the misguided perception that they do not have to worry about heart disease. Actually, when it hits women, usually ten years later, it hits with a vengeance" states Dr. Russell Reeves, a cardiologist with CardioVascular Associates P.C.

It has been believed that women developed heart disease about ten years later than men do because the hormone estrogen protected us from heart disease. However, recent studies are raising questions about this long held belief. Dr. Reeves stated that a recent study by The National Institutes of Health revealed that estrogen replacement therapy does little to reduce the risks of a second heart attack. It now appears that four to five years of therapy is required to reduce the risks for women who have already developed cardiovascular disease. It is best to talk with your physician about the benefits and risks associated with estrogen replacement therapy after menopause. Estrogen may not be recommended for you if you have active liver disease, previous diagnosis of breast or uterine cancer, active gallbladder disease, or a history of blood clots. Caution is also advised for women who already have advanced coronary disease, chronic liver disease, diabetes, hypertension, are severely overweight or have a history of stroke.

Coronary heart disease is the number one killer in the United States with strokes being the number three and most debilitating type of heart disease. Strokes are sometimes referred to as a heart attack of the brain. The vessels in the brain become clogged or have spasms that interrupt the blood supply to a particular area of the brain. Warning signs include: sudden confusion, difficulty speaking or understanding what is being said to them, sudden trouble seeing out of one or both eyes, numbness in one side of the face, numbness in the arm or leg of one side of the body, sudden trouble with balance, walking or coordination, and sudden severe headache.

There are numerous factors that increase the risk of heart disease. You are not in control of your family history, yet this increases your risk also. If you had a parent who had a heart attack before the age of 65 or a sibling who had a heart attack before the age of 55, you are at higher risk. Also, if a close blood relative has suffered a stroke, your risk is higher. It is also believed that African-American women are at greater risks than caucasians. This may be associated with the higher likelihood of elevated blood pressure that is untreated or with the higher percentage of African-American women who live a less active lifestyle and carry excess weight.

Until recent years, heart disease was not considered as likely in women. Perhaps, it is the change in lifestyle over the past thirty years that has increased the numbers of women affected. Women have taken on the stress of highly responsible positions in business and professional arenas. They have been working longer hours, then going home to work a second shift caring for family. Whatever the reason, more women are developing heart disease and it is up to us to make the lifestyle changes needed to reduce these risks.

There are some early warning signs to watch for to prevent heart disease. By watching these markers along the way, women can greatly reduce the risks of heat disease, heart attacks, and stroke.

High Blood Pressure: The person with hypertension is five times more likely to have a heart attack than someone with a normal blood pressure. At age 55, the risk for high blood pressure is about even with men. After age 75, it is estimated that 77% of women have high blood pressure. The blood pressure is the measure for the force of pressure required to push the blood through the arteries. As vessels become clogged or narrowed, more pressure is required. Many people have no symptoms of high pressure. Others report headaches or feeling tense when the pressure rises. The optimal blood pressure is 120/80. A pressure of 140/90 is considered borderline high. Be sure to alert your physician if you find it is running high. This condition can be easily treated.

High cholesterol is another warning sign that you cannot feel and will not know you have unless you get the lab test performed. Cholesterol is a natural substance produced by our bodies to make hormones and vitamin D. There is low density cholesterol (LDL) which comes from animal fats and is the kind you want to keep low. The LDL carries the cholesterol from the liver through the bloodstream and high levels promote the build up of cholesterol in the vessels. High density cholesterol (HDL) carries the blood to the liver where cholesterol can be broken down and removed from the body. It helps some people remember "H is for healthy". Triglycerides are another fatty product that comes from the food we eat. These carry a small amount of cholesterol and tend to run high in women who have a high LDL. Desirable levels of these factors are:

LDL	less than 160 mg/dL
HDL	over 50 mg/dL
Total Cholesterol	under 200 mg/dL
Triglycerides	under 150 mg/dL

Know your numbers to help reduce your risk.

Smoking is a habit we all know is harmful to our health. But if you are a woman with other risk factors for heart disease, it is imperative that you take control where you can. It is

91

estimated that about one-fifth of all cardiovascular illnesses are caused by smoking. Further, two-thirds of heart attacks in women are related to smoking. Cigarette smoking also is the single greatest risk factor for peripheral vascular disease that causes a reduction in the blood flow to the muscles in the arms and legs. If you smoke, it is time to face the facts. Smoking has no positive outcomes. There is no reason to keep smoking and numerous reasons to stop.

Obesity goes hand-in-hand with our more sedentary lifestyles. Weight alone does not give a clear picture of the risks. Body Mass Index or BMI is a rating of weight and height to indicate a more accurate ratio. The desirable BMI is under 25. A rate of 25 to 29 is considered overweight. Over 30 is considered obese.

To calculate your BMI, follow these steps:

1- Multiply your current weight by 703
(Example: 140 pounds x 703=98420)
2- Multiply your height in inches by your height in inches.
(Example: If you are 5'5", you are 65 inches tall. Multiply 65x65=4225)
3- Divide the answer to number 1 by the answer in number 2
(Example: 98420 divided by 1445 = 23.29 rounded to 23)

Your BMI is 23.

If you are overweight, there are ways to reduce your risks through healthy eating and regular exercise. Avoid binge or fad diets. These are not effective in the long run. You need a healthy lifestyle. Long-term lifestyle changes need to be gradually incorporated into your daily routine. Walking for ½ hour a day can lead to overall better cardio-pulmonary health. Increasing the number of vegetables and fruits while cutting back on fats allows one to improve overall diet habits.

It is time for Sara, like many other women to recognize that if she does not care of herself, she may become unable to care for the ones she loves. Taking care of yourself is not a selfish act. It is a necessary responsibility for each woman to take seriously. Take a closer look at your life. Think about letting go of unnecessary roles and activities. Spend time with family and friends who are nurturing and positive. Make time for prayer, reflection, exercise and healthy eating as your priorities. Look for ways to enjoy life more!

Women and Cancer

The primary form of cancer we hear about concerning women is breast cancer. Breast cancer is actually the second most common form women face. Skin cancer leads the pack. Avoiding prolonged exposure to the sun and using sun-screens are the simplest ways to avoid this form of cancer. Products have been developed to protect our skin from the harmful ultraviolet rays, and we should use them. The concept of the tanned beauty is falling out of style, but many of us still believe we look younger and healthier with a bit of a tan. Just be sure that tan isn't causing premature aging or setting you up for skin cancer later in your life.

The American Cancer Society estimates that 192,000 new cases of breast cancer will be diagnosed and 40,800 will die from breast cancer during the next year in the United States alone. Seventy-five percent of women are over the age of fifty when the cancer is found. Nearly eighty percent of women who develop breast cancer have no hereditary link to this disease and therefore are often unaware of the actual risk. Symptoms are often minor and are not found unless a woman is doing breast self-exams. The classic symptoms for breast cancer are:

- lump or mass in the breast
- swelling of a part of the breast
- skin irritation or dimpling
- nipple pain or retraction
- discharge from the nipple other than normal breast milk

The key risk factors are:

Gender: Breast cancer is 100 times more common in women that in men

Aging: Seventy seven percent of women are over the age of 50 when diagnosed

Genetics: Ten percent of breast cancers are related to mutated genes

Family History: Having a first degree (mother, sister, or daughter) relative with the disease doubles the risk

Personal History: If you have had a previous breast cancer the risk is three to four times higher

Race: White women have a higher incidence, yet black women tend to develop the more aggressive types and experience a higher fatality rate

Previous biopsy: There is a higher risk of cancer if previous biopsy revealed an atypical hyperplasia. Fibrocystic changes in the breast are not associated with a higher risk.

Previous Irradiation: There is a significantly higher risk if radiation was used for the treatment of a previous cancer.

Menstrual Periods: If a woman started menstruating before the age of twelve or went through menopause after the age of fifty, there is a slightly higher risk.

Elizabeth Gregory

These are the risks over which we have no control. What can we do to reduce our risks? We can make lifestyle changes to reduce the following risks:

<u>Oral Contraceptive Use</u>: There is a slightly higher risk if a woman was on oral contraceptives for over ten years.

<u>No Pregnancy</u>: A woman who did not have children or had the first child after the age of thirty has a slightly higher risk.

<u>Hormone Replacement Therapy</u>: there may be a slightly higher risk with the use of HRTs

<u>Not breast feeding</u>: Breast feeding may slightly reduce the risk, especially if the mother breast fed for as long as 1.5 to 2 years.

<u>Alcohol Use</u>: Even the ingestion of two to five drinks a day increases the risk by one and a half times.

<u>Obesity/High Fat Diets</u>: Fat tissue can cause the increase in estrogen levels and thereby increase the risks. This risk seems to be higher for women who have gained a significant amount of weight in adulthood as compared to women who were heavy as children.

<u>Physical Inactivity</u>: Even moderate exercise may reduce the risk.

So there we have it again. How many times must we be told to reduce the intake of fat, increase the exercise and avoid alcohol before we take it to heart!

Ovarian Cancer

The American Cancer Society estimates that about one in seventy women will develop ovarian cancer. That's 25,000 women developing cancer and 14,000 dying of this form of cancer in a single year. Half of all these cancers occur in women over the age of 65.

The symptoms of ovarian cancer are:

- Lower abdominal swelling or bloating
- Loss of appetite or feeling full after a small meal
- Gas, indigestion or nausea
- Unexplained weight loss
- Changes in bowel habits to include diarrhea or constipation
- Increased frequency of urination
- Vaginal bleeding—this is actually a rare sign
- Increase fluid around the lungs with shortness of breath

Elizabeth Gregory

The most common risk factors include:

Family History: There is an increase in risk if a family member has been diagnosed. In only about five percent of the cases diagnosed, is there a family history of ovarian cancer.

No Pregnancies: Again, not having children or waiting until after the age of thirty seems to increase the risk

History of Breast Cancer: If a woman has had breast cancer, she is at risk for developing ovarian cancer.

Aging: Again, our risk increases with age. Pap smears are the easiest way to detect any irregular cells from the cervix. Be sure you follow your physician's advice on the frequency of pap smears. Even if you have had a hysterectomy, pap smears are still advised to recognize any early signs of irregular cell growth.

Unfortunately, ovarian cancer symptoms do not appear early and the cancer is already progressed when found. Regular visits with your gynecologist is your best defense.

Recommended web sites for updated information are: www.cancer.org and www.breastcancer.org.

Women and Depression

Another area in which women seem to be affected far more than men is in the realm of emotional illnesses. Depression occurs twice as often in women than in men and there are several theories about why that is the case. Some believe that hormonal fluctuations may be linked to the onset of depression. That explains the incidence of post-partum depression and an increase in depression during menopause. Situational depressions, those brought on by the life situation, may occur more often in women because we feel less free to make life changes needed for our mental health. We are overly concerned sometimes with how those changes will affect others. Major Depression differs from the usual blues any of us can get. Depression lasts at least six months. The blues will pass. Depression does not just go away and you can't just pull yourself up by your bootstraps and keep going. Especially for women of faith, depression carries a negative stigma. The Christian woman will be afraid to admit that she has been down for a long period of time or that she is actually having thoughts of suicide because these feeling may be interpreted as a lack of faith. The common symptoms of a major depressive episode are:

- fatigue
- changes in sleep pattern, either over sleeping or difficulty sleeping
- loss of appetite
- loss of weight
- irritability
- mood swings
- increased awareness of minor physical aches and pains
- negative thinking
- lowered sense of self-esteem
- inability to experience pleasure from things you once enjoyed
- feelings of guilt or worthlessness
- hopelessness
- suicidal thoughts

If you have these symptoms and they have lasted for at least six months, talk to your physician. Consider consulting a mental health professional. The combination of anti-depressant medication and therapy has been shown to be the most effective treatment.

God will surely walk with you through the valleys of depression just as He did with David in the Psalms. But just as with any other issue in your life, you first have to be willing to let God in. Many women express confusion and anger at God when they are depressed. "How could He let this happen to me", "I don't believe He cares at all", are frequent comments. These thoughts are part of the illness. The negative thinking and self-defeating thoughts are part of the pattern. The changes in brain chemistry in depression keep you from thinking in a more positive way. You can counteract many of the symptoms just by recognizing that it is the illness that's talking.

In all these high-risk areas, we as women need to recognize the importance of the basics in self-care. Let's review these again. Which ones are you practicing?

_____ I regularly get at least seven hours of sleep each night

_____ I take time out several times a day to breathe and relax

_____ I eat a healthy diet that is low in fat

_____ I regularly get moderate exercise at least three times a week.

_____ I get regular pap smears and gynecological exams

_____ I perform monthly breast self-exams

_____ I share my feelings with my spouse and at least one other trusted friend

Elizabeth Gregory

Remember, you cannot care for others if you don't care for you!

Chapter Eight

How Can Spirituality Be Simplified?

Proverbs 9:10
The fear of the Lord is the beginning of wisdom, and the knowledge of the Holy One is understanding

Psalm 46:10
Be still and know that I am God;...

Romans 12:4-5
For as we have many members in one body, but all the members do not have the same function, so we, being many, are one body in Christ, and individually members of one another.

What is Spirituality?

This word has become overused and is now largely misunderstood. Some of us immediately think of our religion, a faith in God and the sense of peace that comes from a close relationship with our Heavenly Father. Others have images of Far Eastern or New Age practices. Still others hear this word as an occult term and see witches conjuring up spirits. I work as a professional in mental health and addictions. Spirituality is at the core of recovery from these illnesses. In addiction

103

treatment, spirituality is defined as one's relationship to God, to others and to one's self. There is a distinction between spirituality and religion. Religion is one's involvement with a particular organized system of faith. Spirituality refers to one's personal relationship with God. This relationship with God then directly effects every other relationship as one applies the principles of the twelve steps. The twelve steps closely correlate with the plan of salvation as a means of giving our lives to God's keeping, admitting our wrongs (sins), making amends to others, seeking God's guidance in each day, and then extending ourselves to help others in need. The admission of sins and forgiveness has been reduced in intensity because throughout history, alcoholics and addicts have experienced judgmental attitudes and the lack of understanding about addictions in the church. However, both concepts teach that without a spiritual renewal and trust in God, one cannot live a life free from addictions. Why do I refer to addictions here? Look back at the chapters on material possessions and finances. We all seem to be addicted to something in our culture. We all need God to become the center of our lives instead of allowing other gods to occupy that position. Other gods for you may be drugs or alcohol, food, compulsive shopping, spending, gambling, dependency on others, workaholism, physical appearance, prestige, or countless other compulsive pursuits.

I am a Christian. This means that I accept Jesus as the Son of God and follow His example for living. His life was one of love, acceptance of people for where they were in their life journey, and understanding of sinful behaviors. Even with all His admonitions against pride and judgement of others, many Christians have blocked the chance for others to have a relationship with God through our prideful right-ness and self-righteousness. Many have left the church and given up on a religious belief system because of feeling judged, criticized, and shamed by so-called loving Christians. Jesus called us to love our neighbors and to care for those less fortunate than us. We must first pull the plank from our own eye before removing the splinter from another's. How do we open our eyes to God and become sure of what we believe and how God leads us? There are no new answers here.

The Spiritual Disciplines

Classic religious writings refer to the spiritual disciplines of study, prayer, solitude, meditation, worship, submission and forgiveness. In my own journey, I have found that practice of these disciplines seems to come in seasons. There are times when I thirst for the Word of God and search the scriptures for answers and direction. There are other times where I have experienced an emotional and spiritual desert. It is important at these times to remind ourselves that it is not God who has moved away from us, but we who have distanced from Him. In this time of separation, we need to practice the disciplines and ask God to show us where we turned away. There is often a hidden sinfulness that we have been unwilling to acknowledge or submit to Him. Let's take a closer look at each of these disciplines and how we can incorporate them in our lives.

Prayer: Through praying that He reveal areas we need to turn over to Him, we can grow in self-awareness. Prayer leads us to listen to His guidance. Prayer is not a one-way conversation. If your prayers are simply a list of requests you send to God and expect a quick response, then consider yourself at an early stage of growth in this discipline. We seem to start out praying in much the same way we wrote a letter to Santa Claus in our childhood. "Dear God, I've been good. Please give me...". Even childhood prayers can introduce the concept of intercession. "God bless Mommy and Daddy", is a basic form of intercession. Consider this story: Long ago in a faraway land, a nobleman named Amos was granted his request to go before the King of the Land. He was very concerned about his land being invaded by a foreign people and hoped to gain support of the King to place soldiers in the region for the protection of his people. One of his close friends learned that Amos was granted this audience before the King. The friend asked Amos to present his request for a potion to be brought back for his wife who was suffering from an unexplained illness. The potion was rare and expensive because the plants used grew only in a specific area of the country. Amos agreed to carry his friend's petition to the King. Upon Amos' return to his home, his friend sent a servant over to get the potion. Amos had to admit that he was so focused on his own problems and concerns that he completely forgot to ask the King for the healing potion. The servant carried his message back. The friend's wife died shortly after.

Now, how does this story apply to our prayer lives today? When you have a friend share a concern with you and even ask you to pray for them, do you always remember to lift their petition to the Lord when you come before Him? How many prayers have not been answered because we have failed to honor our agreement to intercede for our friend? This is what intercessory prayer actually is. We claim our friend's need before our heavenly Father. An interesting thing occurs when we intercede for others. We become less focused on our own desires and begin to mature spiritually. Gradually our prayers become prayers of gratitude. As we reflect on all God has already done for us, we can appreciate the gifts and abundance of His love. As we become more grateful, we feel an inner need to know God in a more intimate way. Then we are led to pray by simply spending time with God and abiding in His presence. The relationship grows as we spend more time with God and we are led to study His ways and gain a greater understanding of Him.

Study: Study may be only a daily five-minute reading or it may be an in-depth study on a particular issue or area of scripture. If you have never read the Bible through in a year, I urge you to make a commitment to yourself to do so. There are now Bibles available that have the readings in chronological order or those that combine the usual readings where you can read straight through. These are great if you have not been successful in following through with the skipping around that is required if you follow the 'read the Bible in a year' listings in the back of your regular Bible. The availability of excellent resources for study has increased dramatically in recent years. There is a benefit to studying alone and practicing the discipline of solitude as well. When pondering the study alone, you are not concerned about what to say or how to express your thoughts to others. You can be more reflective at your own pace. Studying with others allows you to hear what other people understand from the same material. You can even come to understand your husband at a deeper level when you study scripture and discuss what you are learning with each other.

Here is a technique that I like to use. It forces me to consider how others may interpret a particular passage. There is always more than one side to any story. To help the scriptures come alive, I have found it helpful to look at stories from various angles by imagining myself in the role of the different characters involved. We need to understand the context in which the story took place, then think through how the event would affect the people involved.

Pick a Story: You may want to start with a story that is familiar to you or try one of these.

Mark 11—the entrance of Jesus into Jerusalem

John 5—the healing of the lame man

John 8; 1-12—saving the adulteress from being stoned by the mob

Matthew 20;1-16—fair payment for the workers in the vineyard.

I have always been drawn to the story of the Samaritan woman at the well and have used it for the sample study in this approach.

<u>Read the Story</u>. Start by reading the story slowly and thoughtfully. You may want to read it aloud and experience it as though you were the narrator. Recall what you have learned about the story or review commentaries to put the events into context.

<u>Identify the characters involved</u>. The primary characters are easy to identify. Become aware of the secondary characters; the people in the crowd, onlookers, the disciples who observed Jesus' actions, those who were opposed to His teachings who heard about the event, those who loved Him and may be concerned for His safety.

<u>Imagine yourself in the role of one of the characters</u>. Allow yourself to identify with that person's thoughts and emotions. How do you believe you would respond if the scene happened to you today?

<u>Shift views</u>. Now move into the role of another character. How would their experience be different from the first person? Would there be a difference in the feelings or reactions?

<u>Apply to your current life.</u> How might this story increase your awareness of how God is at work in the world today? Have you developed an insight as to how actions are interpreted differently depending upon a person's past experience? How can this story help you discern God's will for you today?

110

In using this approach, I have felt God at work in my life by making me more aware of how a person's background may lead them to see the same event quite differently. Our modern day cultural barriers are not so different from those in the days of Christ. I have been able to develop a sensitivity to the perceptions of others and had a better understanding of how others may resist God's call because of past teachings or experiences. This can help me think through how I may reach them in sharing God's word.

An example of how this works is the story of the Samaritan woman meeting Jesus at the well. When this story from the fourth chapter of John has been presented in lessons and sermons, it has been told through the dialogue between Christ and the woman. First, just by reading the story, we can see how Jesus gives her a few clues as to who He is and what He has to offer her. "If you knew the gift of God, and who it is who says to you 'Give me a drink', you would have asked Him and He would have given you living water." (verse 10). "Whoever drinks of this water will thirst again, but whoever drinks of the water that I shall give him will never thirst. But the water that I shall give him will become in him a fountain of water springing up into everlasting life." (verses 13-14)

Well, to Jesus, all that He said was perfectly clear. He knew that He was the wellspring of God's eternal love and power.

Imagine for a moment that you are the woman seeking to understand His strange words. Was this man talking of water? Certainly not any kind of water that she had known of before!

Then when Jesus tells her about herself, she saw Him as a prophet in verse 19. This woman was indeed insightful. She stayed with Him and sought to understand Him. As the story continues, she tells Him that she knows a Messiah is coming and Jesus revealed His identity to her. She was not a Jew, but a Samaritan, yet she believed the story that a Messiah was to come to save His people and she was looking for Him.

This was the first recorded time that Jesus revealed himself...and it was to a woman...and to a Samaritan. Why did He choose her? Imagine her amazement at His words! We are told that she left her waterpot (in her excitement?), went into the city and said to the men in verse 29 "Come, see a Man who told me all things that I ever did. Could this be the Christ?" Perhaps she did not quite trust herself and wanted someone to affirm her belief that Jesus was the Messiah.

Now is the chance to shift views and see the story through the eyes of the men in the town. Who was this woman? She had been married four times and was currently living with a man to whom she was not married. What was it about her proclamation that caused them to take her seriously and go see this man for themselves? Was her face radiant? Was her attitude toward them different? bolder?. There was something that led them to believe that what she said was important. In verse 39, we are told that "And many of the Samaritans of that city believed in Him because of the word of the woman who testified, 'He told me all that I ever did.'" They urged Jesus to stay with them and He agreed. In verse 42, we are told that they had their own personal experience with Christ and after hearing Him for themselves they knew that He was the Christ.

Hallelujah! Jesus can use a woman who is fallen from the accepted traditions of society and bring to Himself even those who probably ridiculed and abandoned her. There is assurance that he can use me too.

Another view to use is that of the disciples. Verse 27 reflects for us that they did not ask what we would expect, "Why are you talking with her?" Instead, they urge Him to eat. Back in verse 6, we see that Jesus is weary from the journey. Had the disciples gone to get food while He sought water? Then Jesus shares with them, "My food is to do the will of Him who sent me, and to finish His work." Did the disciples understand his following statements about harvesting? So often, it seems that those closest to Jesus did not discern His real message. They had seen the baptism of Christ. Yet, this woman of Samaria who had never seen Jesus before, recognized Him readily and He changed her life in a few short moments of conversation.

Are we, who call ourselves disciples, blind to His presence today? Do we recognize His power and position as the Son of God? Are we focused on eating our next meal and missing "the fountain springing up into eternal life"? Let us pray that we can experience the presence of Christ in everyday events in today's world.

There are many ways to focus on scripture and make the stories meaningful to our lives today. I encourage you to seek ways to make study meaningful.

Solitude: The discipline of solitude is a necessity for a woman to be with her Lord and God and to hear His voice over the clamor of the world's demands. Solitude is for most women, a luxury. Yet, if you desire to know God better, it is vital that you practice the discipline of solitude. In our modern society, we can easily block God through the use of television, radio, computers, and staying busy. Some women find that they feel lost and do not know how to just be with God. A few minutes at a time may be all you can do without losing your focus. However, the more you allow yourself to be alone with Him in the quiet, the more comfortable you become. Try walking in early morning or evening for twenty to thirty minutes and just talk with God as you walk. Turn off the car radio and pray on your way to work or the store. Some women become so adept at solitude that they spend days at a time on retreats in complete silence. This is an area where I feel women who are free to be at home all day have an advantage. When the children are down for a nap, use that time to talk to God. Use that time to study and allow Him to keep you calm all through the hectic afternoon. As you feel more comfortable in an intimate relationship with Christ, you will find that you seek solitude simply for the joy of being in His presence.

Meditation: Some people immediately think of far eastern forms of sitting cross-legged and murmuring the same sound over and over. That is helpful for some folks to relax, but it isn't what I am talking about here. The scriptures tell us to meditate on God's word. In Psalm 119:15-16, we are told, "I will meditate on Your precepts and contemplate Your ways. I will delight myself in Your statutes; I will not forget Your word." When you read a passage that seems to speak to you, allow yourself to read it through several times. Write it down and reflect back on it later in the day. Let that passage speak to your soul. Then ask God why He has brought that passage to your attention at this time. It is amazing how often our readings relate directly to a concern on our hearts as we sit down to be with God.

One form of meditation I have enjoyed is to enter a quiet, relaxed state of mind and imagine in my mind's eye that I am in a meadow or on a beach. I can visualize God standing under a tree, or Jesus coming down to me on a cloud. I am then able to be alone with my Lord and just talk with Him in my mind. I can even get a better sense of His answers to my concerns. An interesting thing has happened through the years. When in prayer and meditation before God, my attention has become less focused on my own needs. My prayers have become prayers of praise and gratitude. My petitions are generally in the form of lifting others and their needs to Christ's attention.

Some of us have trouble sitting down for long. You may need to start out in a moving meditation, such as walking prayer. Prayer walking has become popular. Walking alone in your neighborhood and lifting your neighbors to God in prayer is a way of meditation on the concerns in your immediate area. You become more attuned to the needs of others. Two meaningful forms of prayer and meditation that I have learned in recent years are the use of the labyrinth and praying the rosary.

The labyrinth is a twisting turning path that always leads to the center of the circle where one meditates before God. It is representative of the Middle Ages journey to the cathedrals of Europe. There are times when you are walking with your back to the center, yet are moving closer to it at the same time. This practice reflects our walk with the Lord and was a very powerful experience for me. A meditation on this experience follows this chapter.

The rosary is a meditative prayer that also developed in the Middle Ages as villagers yearned to find the same peaceful spirituality of the monks. They began by counting a stone for each prayer or recitation of a psalm. Since the average person could not read, the phrases were shortened to allow memorization and repetition was helpful. Later, the stones began to be placed on a rope with knots tied between them and gradually these were shortened from 150 prayers to fifty. The Catholic tradition introduced the "Hail Mary" as a prayer to be used with meditation on various events in the life of Christ. I had to seek an understanding of these prayers when I began to be drawn to the rosary. Protestant teaching does not elevate Mary's standing in any way and the rosary may appear to go against beliefs we are taught. As in all areas of faith practice, each seeker must reach out to God for guidance in these matters. The meditation on this practice also follows at the end of this chapter.

Worship can be done in solitude, but we also need the company of other Christians to help us grow as well. Time spent with other believers is essential to strengthen our faith.

117

We often use the term, 'church family'. If you have experienced a major loss in your life, you may have come to understand how much your church becomes your family of support in hard times. When both my parents died within ten months, my church family touched my heart more than I can express. They helped hold me together through my grief. Their cards and donations were tangible proof that my parents' lives had made a difference in the world. Somehow, their care for me helped me feel a little less empty inside.

Submission to the Lordship of Christ is a daily act. Many of us have a tendency to take back the control of our lives within a few hours of the time we prayed for Him to direct us. Submission is a conscious and deliberate act. We may submit most areas of our lives to Him, but hold back our secret desires. He cannot work in our lives until we submit everything; every dream, every fear, every sorrow, every joy and every secret part of ourselves to His keeping. He really does know us and knows the secrets of our hearts anyway. Why not just be open about things with Him. There is a wonderful freedom in submission. It is easy to submit small things to Him. But, sometimes there are large areas of our past that we cling to even though that clinging is self-destructive. This leads us to the need for forgiveness.

Forgiveness: The inability to forgive holds many believers in bondage to the past. Some of us need to forgive ourselves. Some of us need to forgive others. There have been entire volumes written just on the discipline of forgiveness, so I will only touch on this act of faith. Forgiveness is for the one doing the forgiving, not for the one who committed the wrong. Chances are that the one you have been unable to forgive, does not even know that you hold a bitterness against them, nor would they care. Take the case of childhood sexual abuse. To hold onto the anger and resentment actually keeps the one who abused you as a child to be in control of your life as an adult. Forgiving them is the only way you can move into a life of freedom. Forgiveness does not mean that you agree with or condone their behavior. If that person is still a part of your life, you may want to let them know that you are forgiving them for your own benefit. However, you do not condone their acts, nor will you sit idly by and allow them to abuse another child. You have made the decision to be a victim no longer.

Self-forgiveness is probably one of the most difficult acts of submission for us to do. There are times when a woman seems to need to hold on to anger, guilt or self-punishment as though it were a badge of honor. Well, it isn't a medal of glory. It is simply a refusal to allow God into that area of our lives and wipe the slate clean. After all, He promised us that our sins are

Elizabeth Gregory

forgiven and they are as far away as the east is from the west. If we keep bringing up our past sins, how can God forget about them? Another phrase to recall is the statement of The Lord's Prayer in which we ask that God forgive us our trespasses as we forgive the trespasses of others against us. It may be that we cannot experience God's forgiveness in our spirit until we let go of all old resentments. Forgiveness is not an emotion, it is an act of faith.

Now let's do a little more self-assessment. How do you currently practice the following disciplines?

Study:

Prayer:

Meditation:

Solitude:

Submission:

Worship:

Forgiveness:

How do you desire to grow in the practice of these disciplines?

In The Christian's Secret Of A Happy Life, Hannah Whitall Smith stated, "The greatest burden we have to carry in life is self; the most difficult thing we have to manage is self... You must hand yourself, with your temptations, your temperament, your frames and feelings, and all your inward and outward experiences, over into the care and keeping of God, and leave it all there. He made you, and therefore understands you, and knows how to manage you; and you must trust him to do it."

How Can Women Help Each Other?

In my experience, one of the downfalls of women's groups in the church has been this. The first thirty to forty-five minutes is spent in "fellowship", or rather gossip time. The gossip may be sugar coated with, "Did you hear about Doris, poor thing. We really must pray for her." In all sincerity, was the point in telling the story really to ask for prayer or to tell on Doris and her troubles? When we focus on honest sharing about ourselves instead of expounding on the troubles of others in a gossipy fashion, we may well be nearing true spiritual growth. In twelve step fellowships like Alcoholics Anonymous one is reminded to take your own inventory. In other words, it is not your job to determine how another person should be living their life. If you start thinking you can do it better than they can, you are experiencing pride, and pride my friend, leads to the fall. Chances are you will be the next one everyone is talking about! One of the most hurtful experiences in my life was following a painful divorce when I attended a women's study group in a home I had never entered before. The study was on relationships and I began to uncontrollably cry as my grief hit the surface. I literally did not know where the bathroom or kitchen were located and could not gain control of myself to either leave the room or stop crying. Everyone in the group study, women who had known me for years, pretended nothing was happening. No one stopped to ask if I was alright. No response at all. I am sure they were embarrassed also and just tried to keep me from being embarrassed by giving any attention to the matter. But the feeling I was left with is that others could not handle my pain and did not care enough to help me carry that burden. Why are we so afraid to show love and concern to the hurting people in our midst? Was it more important to be sure and cover the lesson material than to help in the healing of a hurting person? I left that church. No one ever called to inquire why and whether I was worshipping elsewhere. If we are filled with the love of Christ for others, can you imagine allowing this scene to be repeated?

Getting To Know You

The basic foundation of any relationship is to get to know the other person and to allow them to know you. We need to know God if we are going to have a closer walk with Him. He has provided many resources for us. We are surrounded by His creation. We have the Scriptures to study and through which to seek His heart. We have opportunities to learn of the faith from others who are more mature in the spirit. How does any friendship develop? By spending time together. Check this list out. Which ones apply to your time with God?

_____ I spend time studying God's word on a regular basis

_____ I tell God my fears and concerns

_____ I share my hopes and dreams with my Heavenly Father

_____ I trust His judgement more than my own

_____ I am able to be still and just be with Him

_____ I am clear about God's overall purpose in my life

_____ When making a major decision, I ask God for guidance

_____ I see God's hand at work in the world around me

_____ I am willing to be God's hands, His feet and His voice in the world today

_____ I have confessed the deepest sins of my soul, asked for and have accepted God's forgiveness

_____ I have a strong desire to know God even better

A healthy relationship is one built on trust, respect and honesty. How healthy is your relationship with God? He is all those things. Are you being open, honest, truthful, and respectful with Him?

When we are firmly grounded in our relationship to God as father, Jesus as teacher, brother and friend and can allow the Holy Spirit to guide us, all other relationships fall into their proper place. That does not mean the life is easy or problem free. It just means that God is there to guide us in all relationships and in every circumstance. Spiritual growth and development are a highly personal experience. It starts with a one to one relationship with Christ. As we are filled by the Spirit, then the fruits of the spirit are manifested in us. When we follow God's guidance everyday, we become loving, joyful, peaceful, patient, kind, good, faithful, gentle and self-controlled. (Galatians 5:22). Others are then drawn to the Spirit. They are not drawn to us as persons, lest we should boast, but are drawn to the Spirit of Christ in us. So, when we receive some recognition or praise for being the woman God created us to be, we must recognize that the glory is not ours, but His.

How are you seeing the fruits of the Spirit growing within you?

What do you need to turn over to God for Him to be able to mold you into the vessel He intends you to be?

God has had quite a challenge molding me into the vessel for His use. I am no perfect follower of His way. I would say I have been more like a wild horse having to be reigned in on numerous occasions. I would rear up and go my own way, not content to wait upon the Lord and thinking I know what is best. After all, I'm a reasonably intelligent woman. Well, I've been wrong every time I took off in my own direction instead of His. Thank God, He has been patient with me! I have grown and am now willing to wait for His direction and I can now trust in His ways.

Caring For You

When I realize I am His creation and He has a purpose for me, it becomes easier to treat myself with respect as well. If He loves and commands that I love my neighbor as myself, then I learn that loving myself is also ordained by God. How do we love ourselves? Here's another checklist to get you started.

_____ I accept myself as an imperfect being

_____ I forgive myself when I make mistakes

_____ I treat my body with respect

_____ I eat a healthy diet

_____ I exercise regularly

_____ I seek medical care when needed

_____ I recognize and accept my emotions as a natural part of me

_____ I seek emotional support as needed

_____ I accept that I am worthy of the respect of others

_____ I spend time with other believers in Christ

_____ I share my prayer concerns

_____ I accept the love of others

_____ I take advantage of opportunities to learn new skills

_____ I set limits with others to allow time and energy for continued spiritual growth

If you are saying "Yes" to these, then you are learning to love yourself. When you take care of yourself, you are happier and more able to reach out to others.

When we are focused on God's desires instead of our own, we can experience a deeper sense of gratitude for all He has done in our lives. Even the hard times, the times we thought we would never live through, have served to make us stronger and more understanding toward others in crisis. God promised, *"Those who sow in tears Shall reap in joy. He who continually goes forth weeping, Bearing seed for sowing, Shall doubtless come again with rejoicing, bringing His sheaves with him."*

(Psalm 126:5-6). May we be dedicated to pursuing the work God has called us to do in the world today.

Discerning God's Purposes in Your Life

How do you know what God is calling you to do? Remember, back in chapter one, I asked if there were any dreams you have had even since childhood? That may be God's calling to you. He gives us gifts to serve Him. He has placed these things in your heart for a reason...to serve Him. Let's take a look at the spiritual gifts as presented in the scriptures. From Romans 12:6-8, "*Having then gifts differing according to the grace that is given to us, let us use them: if prophecy, let us prophesy in proportion to our faith; or ministry, let us use it in our ministering; he who teaches, in teaching; he who exhorts, in exhortation; he who gives, with liberality; he who leads, with diligence; he who shows mercy, with cheerfulness.*"

What gifts do you possess? What passions run deep in your soul? Taking a closer look at the gifts and what they may mean in today's world may help you in understanding God's call in your life. So let's take a closer look.

An apostle is defined as a leader, outstanding figure, or a commissioner to Christ. What traits will a leader who leads others to Christ and confirms them in the faith possess? Is this a part of your calling? Are you being called to serve on a mission field? You may receive the calling to be an apostle of the Word to a foreign country and reach people who have never had the benefit of religious teaching. You may be called to serve on a short-term mission trip either abroad or here in your own country. The church membership has declined in the United States greatly since post World War II days. Other countries are sending missionaries to the United States because we are seen as a rich mission field. Many in our own society have a sense of apathy about religion and see no reason to seek God. We are all surrounded by a mission field and opportunities to witness through word and deed every day. Are you feeling a call to share your faith?

Do you find that people follow your advice and trust you? If so, you have a heavy burden. You must not mislead them. Do you believe you are called as an apostle to reach others for Christ? If so, how are you called to act and what is required to be prepared for this service?

A prophet is one who sees the correct interpretation of God's word and the world events related to the Word. Do you have the gift of discernment and an ability to lead others to see what is happening in a given situation to better understand how God is working in the world? Jerry Jenkins and Tim La Haye may be serving as prophets now to prepare us for the future. In their <u>Left Behind</u> series which is fictional account of the tribulation days prior to Christ's return, they are sharing their view of events based on their own understanding through study of the scriptures and as led by the Spirit. There are certainly several people who have sought to predict the end of days. How will we know whom to believe? That is another subject altogether.

There may be a societal or moral problem in the world that you believe you understand better then others. Do you feel the Spirit nudging you to speak up? You may feel strongly about an ethical situation in your community or our country. Are you being called to work for the kingdom in the capacity of a prophet? If, so, how?

A teacher is one gifted at imparting knowledge to another. The teacher must first have a thorough knowledge base in the subject matter and be able to make it come to life in a way that it has real meaning to the individual being taught. It is not enough to want to teach. It requires a gift. Some of us are gifted at teaching young children, some at working with adolescents and others can only reach adults. Accept the part of the gift for which you are called. Are you called to be a teacher? If so, in what capacity do you feel called to work? How do you need to prepare?

Now a worker of miracles is rare indeed, and we are skeptical of anyone who claims to do miraculous things. Perhaps, God works small miracles through any one of us at a specific time when we surrender to Him and fulfill a particular calling. There may be some who can perform miraculous things. Healings that occur through the use of medical advances are still miracles. It is still a miracle when a woman who has spent her life downcast, finds hope in the faith of another believer and is led to that hope by claiming Christ's promises for herself.

Healers are many in our culture. We have those involved in physical healing through the advance of medical science, as well as those who heal damaged emotions and spiritual scars. Are you called to work with people in physical, emotional or spiritual pain? Do you have an unusual capacity to understand those that the world has cast out? Even in the area of nursing, there are those of us who feel a call to work with persons suffering emotional illnesses and addictions. Others are called to work with victims of cancer and assist in their recovery or help them to prepare for their death. Still others minister to the new mother as she adjusts to her role as caretaker of a fragile and dependent infant. If you feel you are called to work with hurting people, it may be wise to talk to those who work in the area to which you are feeling called. They can help you clarify whether this is a calling or just a desire to do a specific job based on an idea you have about the work. Sometimes, when you learn the reality of the work, the desire no longer lingers. Are you called to be a healer? What area are you called for and what is required to prepare you to do this work competently?

We need helpers in every aspect of life. We can all serve as helpers in some capacity. Cleaning up after a fellowship dinner, keeping the children in the nursery, leading the singing, assisting in the campaign of an honest politician, and volunteering at a local organization are all examples of helping. You will not be likely to hear a booming voice from on high telling you where to serve. You may feel a compelling need to help in a special ministry. Even if you do not believe you have a particular gift, God may call you in a moment's flash to help out a stranger in need or donate to a special cause. We are all helpers. How do you serve as a helper?

Do you have the gifts of organizational ability, writing, speaking, accounting, building maintenance, leading committees, motivating others or sharing a vision? You may be called upon to serve in the governing of your church, a community organization or in your work. We need people with leadership skills that are willing to work behind the scenes to get many jobs done for society and churches to meet the needs of people. Are you called to serve by sharing your organizational and leadership skills? What skills do you possess that can be used in this way?

A diversity in languages is highly desired today. There are some who believe in the concept of speaking in tongues taught by some churches. There are places where knowledge of other languages is greatly needed. With the influx of Hispanics to the United States, there is a need for teachers of Spanish for health care workers and schools. There is a need for those who can teach English as a second language. The deaf in our culture still live a world outside the mainstream of society because so few of us can talk with those who speak another language. When they enter an office for services or enter the hospital for medical care, qualified interpreters are needed to assure they understand the processes they are experiencing. Can you imagine going into an emergency room in a foreign country where no one spoke your language? You are in critical need of help and your life could be in danger. This is what people from other cultures experience on a daily basis. There are many in our communities who cannot read or write the English language effectively. Are you gifted at making words come to life and motivating someone to an improved literacy? Are you gifted in the area of languages or tongues? How are you called to serve?

There are many gifts given by God to build up the body of Christ. The gifts of music, of being a good listener, of caring enough to prepare a casserole for a sick friend or neighbor and to keep a child for a friend who needs a break are all valid areas of service. We are all a part of the body of Christ. The mouth is no more important than the big toe. All parts are needed. If you have a gift that God is calling you to use, be aware that we all need you. In what ways are you called to assist others?

Susan Whitley, a lay leader with the Baptist Church in north Alabama has been included in many mission trips both in this country and to Australia, Africa, the Philippines and South America. She shared her view about being gifted and serving in missions, "Many people do not recognize their own gifts. They don't know how they can help. But we are all given a gift, we just have to be willing to allow God to use us. They need to understand that they are not making a trip on their own power, but it's the power of God using them. That's what is making the difference."

To be His hands, His feet and His voice, we must first seek simplicity and place God first. If we are running in all directions trying to do all things for all people, we will be useless to God. We must slow down and hear His call before we act. We must also remember that *"And though I have the gift of prophecy, and understand all mysteries and all knowledge, and though I have all faith, so that I could remove mountains, but have not love, I am nothing.* "(I Corinthians 13:2)

Now that you have taken a look at the various areas of spiritual service, what are you feeling called to do?

Do you have the background and preparation to do this task? Is there specific training you need to pursue this area of service?

In the next chapter, we will attempt to review all this in-depth self-evaluation and pull it all together in a way that you can apply these principles to your life today.

The Labyrinth

I stood in the doorway, soaking in the effects of candlelight
surrounding the labyrinth.
The dark panels of wood on the lower walls illuminated.
The cross in the center of the far wall in shadows.

Moving inside the room, I was pulled to the safety of watching
other pilgrims
embarking on their journey to the Holy Land, to the heart of
God.
Two had begun their journey, a woman and a man walking the
labyrinth together,
yet each alone.
How like life.
We each walk the journey of life, alone.
Yet we share our world with so many others.
These two, never speaking, nor making any connection to one
another.
Each deep within themselves.

I approached the labyrinth, hesitated, took a deep breath, and
stepped inside.
It was as though I feared this journey.
What kind of power does the labyrinth possess?
Would I be the same when I emerged?
I said to my soul "I am here, now guide me."
Allowing thoughts to wander and feelings to flow,
I immersed myself in this new experience.

One cannot discern the path at the first step.
One can only follow, trusting it will lead to the center and out
again.

Elizabeth Gregory

Moving slowly, arms wrapped about myself in a hugging
embrace, I walked.
The twists and turns are so like life.
never knowing when life will change
nor where it will lead next.
Some straight-aways are short, others longer.
Some are close to the center and others move away from it.
Again, what a metaphor for my walk with you God.
There are times when I feel so close to you,
other times I turn my back and walk another way, feeling
distant and disconnected.
The center never moves, only I do.
Even when walking away, I am coming closer to the center.
Is that how life is Lord?
My turning away from you being part of the process of finding
you?

I pass others, we turn, so our bodies will not touch.
We look down, and away.
Most others we pass in this journey of life remain anonymous.

I am aware of how the labyrinth is speaking to me...more in
questions than in answers.
Why do we close each other out?
Is it allowed to look into the eyes of another?
We are all here for the journey.
We all share a common desire.
yet each has our own need.

Tears begin to form.
Then, she steps up, looks into my eyes with hands held, ready
to touch.
I take her hands, lean forward and whisper, "thank you".
We smile and continue our walking.
The tears begin to fall.

Feeling the connection to another human can be so powerful.
A woman of grace, sharing love calmly, with no expectation
has a healing influence.
Lord, let me accept what she offers.
Lord, help me to be that inspiration for others.

I have no concept of how far I have come.
Is reaching the center halfway?
Or is it all the way?
Am I halfway through my life?
Or did life cease to be measurable when Christ brought me
eternity?

Most travelers moved slowly.
I also kept the pace slow and calm in this meandering path.
Then, I realized, this next turn leads to the center.
I stepped into the center, moved to the arc on the far side and
looked upward.
There, on the wall in shadows was the cross.
I stood and prayed.
I am so full of questions Father. I seek answers,
Perhaps there are none.
I seek to know you with a longing so intense I have no words
to describe it.
I have always sought you, even as a child, in solitude and
quiet.
I contemplate your ways, hoping for understanding.
Help me to trust you more.
Guide my every step towards you.
Lead me when I leave this center, to keep you with me.
Allow me to experience your heart in all places.
Allow me to know your love at all times.
Teach me to be your love for those who are wandering through
this world,
with no awareness of the center.

Turning, I see the light of candles on tall, thin black poles.
I recall the medieval uses of the labyrinth.
I watch the others on their journeys.
I silently pray for each of them to find what they are seeking.

Thoughts come, unevoked.
We have always had suffering.
Poverty is always present on this earth.
Wars, hatred, misunderstandings have occurred all through the
history of mankind.
Do we need these experiences to learn?
Are they all a part of the journey?
Do we create them when we cannot see the center?
The journey back commences.

Each has to follow their own path.
You have only to walk yours.
Those you love will walk theirs.
Your friends will follow their own paths.
Your colleagues each have their own journeys.
You need only walk yours.
You need only walk yours.
You need not walk for someone else.
You cannot walk their journey for them.
Each must walk one's own path.
You need walk only yours.

I am lighter, freed of the burden of feeling responsible for
others.
Trusting in my soul to lead me,
Resting in the knowledge and experience of God as father,
Following the guidance of Jesus, the Christ.
I must walk only my path.

Our paths converge again, we embrace.
There is such beauty when one life touches another,
Each walking our own paths.
Our contact may be brief, paths may never cross again,
But that moment is real...and profound.

Few travelers notice each other.
That too, is part of the journey,
Boundaries respected, and trusted.

The end was only a few feet away.
I was not ready for the end.
I stood at the exit, breathed deeply, and prayed,
Lord, let me keep you as the center as I leave this place.
Reside in my heart and help me to dwell in yours.
Let me feel your loving embrace.
Let me show your love to others on this journey
of life. Amen

The Sorrowful Mysteries

It began during Advent, this attraction to the rosary
with a calling to a form of meditative prayer.
I did not know the history or the meaning
and so a search began.
In medieval times, the monks said their prayers through the
psalms
and peasants longed for the spiritual path.
They began by recitations counted on stones, then tied the
stones together.
The early rosary was begun.
"Hail Mary, full of grace"
a new concept to an old protestant.
Mary? without sin? Yet, God chose her out of all the women on
earth to be the mother of His beloved son.
She must have possessed special qualities.
Did he set her apart from her birth, protect her from the sin of
the world around her and prepare her for this special part she
was to play in the life of Christ...and all Christians?
"The Lord is with thee. Blessed art thou among women.
Blessed is the fruit of thy womb, Jesus."
Only scripture quoted here.
"Holy Mary, mother of God" ...of God.
If God and Christ are one, then she is the mother of God.
"Pray for us sinners."
I have no problem claiming my sinfulness.
Mary, pray for me. This is only a desire for a dear friend, the
mother of us all to talk to her Son, or to God on my behalf.
Yes, I do ask earthly friends to pray for me...why not the Saints
who share heaven with my Lord?
"Now and at the hour of our death."
There is another distinction in theology.
Does anyone need to pray me to heaven? The blood of Christ
paved the way.

Then again, do I have any problem with Mary saying a prayer on my behalf that my Father receive me in His heavenly kingdom?
Surely the minister will be doing the same at my funeral.
As I struggle with the concept of Hail Mary's, I find that there are no barriers to praying to the saints within my own personal theology.
And so the journey continues.

Lent, a time of deep reflection on the passion of Christ.
The sorrowful mysteries...a walk through the last week of Christ's life.
A meditation on his prayer in the garden and of His willingness to be our sacrificial lamb.
The betrayal of Judas, the denial of Peter,
how alone my Lord was as He faced Pilate.
The scourging, they beat my Jesus.
The tears fall every time I meditate on thirty lashings with a whip.
"Through His stripes we are healed."
The crown of thorns.
They mocked Him, placing a crown of thorns upon his brow and calling him king.
They made fun of this man and Lord I have worshipped all my life.
How could they treat Him so?
Yet, do I not mock Him every time I refuse to seek Him and go my own way?
Do I not deny Him just as Peter did when I fail to stand up for my faith?
The carrying of the cross.
Here the gospels are in disagreement. Did He carry His own cross or not?
All agree that Simon helped Him.
Would I have taken up His cross to spare Him pain?

143

Elizabeth Gregory

Do I take up His cross today?
The crucifixion. Oh My God!
The pain you endured for all of us who are incapable of
appreciating your efforts to reach us.
As I repeat the Hail Mary's, I think of her during these times.
To see her son mocked, shamed, beaten, crucified and dying.
Oh Mary, did you know the pain ahead when you said yes to
Gabriel?
Did you know you would see him die?
The rosary, a meditative prayer
that did indeed make this the most meaningful Lenten season I
have experienced.
Then, after His death, the glorious mysteries come to light.
A new season in the life of a seeking Christian.

Chapter Nine

Living The Abundant Life

John 10:9-10
I am the door. If anyone enters by me, he will be saved, and will go in and out and find pasture. The thief does not come except to steal, and to kill, and to destroy. I have come that they may have life, and that they may have it more abundantly.

Reading to gain knowledge allows you to learn a few things. If it is your desire to make the discipline of simplicity a reality, you must put knowledge into action. You have answered questions and hopefully given some serious thought to how you manage your life. Now, let's put all this into action by setting specific goals. Start by taking time to be alone with God. Enter into prayer and ask that He guide you as you answer the following questions to set your goals. Do not go through this process in a hurried fashion. Listen for the guidance of the Holy Spirit.

Chapter One—Where Do I Start?

1—What will it mean to you to simplify your life?

2—Who are you? Have you gained a clearer image of the woman that God created you to be? Describe yourself here:

3—Describe any circumstance that is causing you to currently re-define your roles and relationships:

4—What dreams have you had since childhood? What passions and interests has God placed within you to allow you to serve and glorify Him?

5—How will you put these into action now?

Chapter Two—Where Does All the Time Go?

1—How do you intend to use your time differently?

2—What stage of life are you presently living?

_____ single woman   _____ caring for aging parents

_____ young wife   _____ experiencing a new mid-life freedom

_____ wife and mother   _____ passing mid-life

_____ step-mother   _____ looking toward retirement

_____ single parent   _____ retired

_____ mid-life   _____ aging

_____ children are grown

3—How does this season influence the time available to you to pursue your own dreams?

4—What is God calling you to do in this season?

5—What ideas did you learn for simplifying household tasks and work responsibilities?

Elizabeth Gregory

6—What is the greatest lesson you have learned about the seasons of your life and how God works through the life cycles?

Chapter Three—Is All This Activity Really Necessary?

1—How can you separate work responsibilities from home activities?

2—In doing the schedules and charts included in this chapter, what did you learn about the activities that fill your days?

3—What ideas about organizing work and family activities will you use to help you simplify your life?

4—What activities do you need to discontinue?

5—What is one activity that you can add for the sheer enjoyment or creativity?

6—What will you teach your children about simplifying activities?

7—Are you an extrovert or introvert?

8—What actions must you take to balance quiet time and time with others?

9—How can you balance active and sedentary activities?

Chapter Four—What Am I Supposed to Do With All This Stuff?

1—What goals are you ready to set to reduce the clutter in your life?

2—What did you learn about your shopping and spending habits that prevent you from simplifying your life?

3—What possessions no longer "fit" the woman you have become? What can you do with these things?

4—What electronic devices are complicating your life? What steps must you take to regain control?

Chapter Five—How Can Managing My Money Simplify My Life?

1—Which danger signs of financial difficulties did you check?

2—What steps are you prepared to take to reduce the clutter of debt in your life?

3—How do you feel God is leading you to support the work of His kingdom through the church, missions and community organizations? What amount can you commit to this work at present?

4—What subscriptions and memberships do you need to end in order to reduce unnecessary spending?

5—If you are raising children or assisting with grandchildren, what do you plan to teach them about the proper use of money?

Chapter Six—How On Earth Do You Simplify Relationships?

1—Who were the people that encouraged you and what was the impact they made upon you as a child?

2—How can you show your gratitude?

3—What children can you influence now? How will you be that encourager for them?

4—What will you do to improve the quality of one deep friendship?

5—What relationships do you need to "let go"?

6—How can you, in your church and community, reach out to assist single parents?

7—If you are divorced, what are you doing to encourage a healthy relationship between your child and your ex-spouse?

8—If you are married, is this relationship supportive and nourishing for both of you?

9—Are there areas of conflict that require marriage mentoring or professional guidance? If so, who will you seek to help you?

10—What are you doing to show your husband that you love and cherish him?

11—What do you need your husband to do to assure that you feel loved and cherished by him? How will you tell him these things?

12—How will you invite God into your relationship with your spouse?

Chapter Seven—Taking Care of You

1—Which risk factors do you have for heart disease?

2—What will you do to reduce your risks for cardiovascular disease?

3—Which risk factors do you have for breast or ovarian cancer?

4—What measures will you take to reduce your risks of cancer?

5—How high a risk do you have for experiencing depression?

6—What will you do to reduce these risks?

Chapter Eight—How Can Spirituality Be Simplified?

1—How do others know that you are a Christian?

Elizabeth Gregory

2—What are you doing to enrich and deepen your relationship with God?

3—Which spiritual disciplines do you practice regularly?
_____ study   _____ stewardship
_____ prayer   _____ simplicity
_____ meditation   _____ fasting
_____ submission   _____ solitude
_____ worship   _____ others?

4—Which discipline do you plan to further develop at this time?

5—What fruits of the spirit (love, joy, peace, patience, faithfulness, gentleness, self-control) do you desire to experience? How can God manifest these in your life?

6—What fruits of the spirit do you believe you now possess that draw others to Christ in you?

7—How do you create obstacles to keep God from molding you into a vessel for His use?

8—What gifts (apostle, prophecy, teaching, miracle worker, healer, helper, organizer, tongues, others) has God given you and how do you plan to use these to further His kingdom?

9—How do you need to prepare to use these gifts to do His work?

10—What will you do differently to love and care for yourself?

Elizabeth Gregory

Conclusion:

You have now clarified goals in each area we have studied. I encourage you to begin the work of simplifying your life. Yes, that's right. You are just beginning the process at this point. When you reach your goals, you will find a richer, more meaningful life. You cannot do this work alone. You can only find God's purpose for your life in union with Him. You can only live a more focused and simplified life when you daily submit to His will and stay aware of how the world's values pull you away from your relationship with your Heavenly Father.

Think through every purchase, every activity and every relationship. Ask Him to show you how each decision fits into the whole tapestry He has woven for you...and you alone. Now, one final exercise. Write a letter to yourself that describes what you have learned by studying this book. In your letter, state what goals you have set and how you plan to simplify your life while drawing closer to God. Place the letter is a self-addressed, sealed envelope and give it to a trusted friend with the instruction to mail it to you in six months. That will force you to review your goals when you receive that letter and renew your commitment. May God bless you richly as you grow in spiritual maturity.

About the Author

Elizabeth C. Gregory is a writer and seminar leader who specializes in the areas of emotional health and spiritual growth.

She works as Program Director of behavioral health services at Baptist Medical Center—Montclair in Birmingham, Alabama.

Elizabeth is highly credentialed in her field with licensure as a Psychiatric Nurse Clinical Specialist and Licensed Professional Counselor. She is also certified as a master's level addiction professional and is board certified as a national certified counselor.

She has published over a hundred articles in periodicals for which she regularly writes in the Birmingham area as well as some national publications. She writes a bi-weekly column, 'Get a Grip' in *The Leeds News*.

Local television stations, radio programs, and newspapers frequently call upon Elizabeth for interviews about topics in her fields of expertise.

Elizabeth is married to John Gregory. John graduated from seminary at Vanderbilt University and serves as a hospital Chaplain. They are active members of Valley Christian Church.

Between them, they have three adult children; Chris, Brian, and Rebecca.

If your church or community organization sponsors retreats and would be interested in having the program from this book or related material presented, you can reach Elizabeth at

2407 Stewart Road SW
Leeds, Alabama 35094
(205) 699-4929

Printed in the United States
1435500006B/212

9 781403 301192